A SCHOOL WITH A VIEW

A History of Ardingly College 1858–2008

A SCHOOL WITH A VIEW

A History of Ardingly College 1858–2008

David Gibbs

The Terrace and beyond.

DEDICATION

This book is dedicated to Nigel Argent, whose research and enthusiasm made it all possible.

A SCHOOL WITH A VIEW:
A HISTORY OF ARDINGLY COLLEGE 1858–2008

Copyright © Ardingly College

First published in 2008 by James and James (Publishers) Ltd,
a member of Third Millennium Information Group

2–5 Benjamin Street
London
United Kingdom
EC1M 5QL
www.tmiltd.com

ISBN: 978 1 903942 83 3

British Library Cataloguing in Publication Data
A CIP catalogue record for this book is available from the British Library.

Project editor: Susan Millership
Designer: Susan Pugsley
Production manager: Bonnie Murray

Reprographics: Asia Graphic Printing Ltd
Printer: Butler and Tanner, Frome, Somerset

Contents

Author Acknowledgements

In 2008 Ardingly College celebrates its 150th anniversary. In some respects it is similar to many other independent schools in the British Isles – 700 boys and girls in three separate, though related, parts (Pre-Prep, Prep and Senior); half-day and half-boarding; typical fees for schools of this kind; a well-balanced education, combining an academic heart with music, drama, sport and adventurous activities; some well- appointed facilities in a rural setting; membership of the Headmasters' and Headmistresses' Conference affirming its position among the leading 250 independent schools in the land. There is nothing here that is out of the ordinary.

Yet Ardingly's origins are anything but typical. St Saviour's School, in due course to be known as Ardingly College, was founded at Shoreham on the Sussex coast in 1858 by a determined, far-sighted and characteristically Victorian churchman, Nathaniel Woodard. Ardingly was to be the heart, indeed 'the jewel in the crown', of a national network of schools designed to reform the moral standing of the nation; and to enable the Church of England to regain the ground lost to the Nonconformists and secularists.

There have been three historians of Ardingly. Dr Reginald Perry taught at the School from 1926 to 1934 and was later a headmaster in the West Country. His scholarly and readable account – *Ardingly 1858–1946: A History of the School* – was published by the Old Ardinians Society in 1951. Stanford Letts, a long-serving member of the School Council and sometime President of the Old Ardinians, wrote a delightful and pertinent book – *Ardingly: Its Building and Buildings* – which was published by the Society in 1985. And finally Nigel Argent, who taught at the School from 1956 until 1982, brought Perry's work up to date with his thematic account – *Ardingly College 1939 –1990*. In addition he edited a fascinating collection of reminiscences of former pupils and staff – *The Ardingly I Remember* – published by the School in 1994.

The aim of this book is not only to bring these accounts up to date, but also to consider as a whole the first 150 years of this remarkable school.

Who was the Founder? How did Ardingly fit into the national picture? How has it overcome all manner of problems created in its first 100 years by chronic under funding? And how has it adapted to a very different role from that which the Founder intended?

One day in the autumn of 2000 Nigel Argent came to Chigwell (where I was then Headmaster) to visit his childhood home, Grange Court. We had a very happy day and talked much about Ardingly and in particular the need for a sesquicentenary history eight years ahead. 'I will be too old for that,' he said, 'you must take it on'. And so here I am! Two days later his son, John, phoned to say that his father had died peacefully at home. This book is dedicated to Nigel.

I have been assisted by many people: the ever helpful Andrea King, Archivist at the College; Gesa Paulfeierborn, who has steered the project through with great patience at the College end; Susan Millership at James & James has been a highly professional and supportive editor; and I have valued the skilful design work of her colleague Susan Pugsley and Sarah Campbell's typing has been meticulous. I am grateful to Headmaster, John Franklin and Chairman of the Council, Robert Alston for supporting the project from the outset. Many Ardinians have written in with their reminiscences. I have enjoyed reading them all and I am only sorry that it has not been possible to use everything sent in.

It goes without saying that any errors are mine.

Foreword

It is a great honour to be writing this foreword approaching Ardingly's 150th anniversary. I have inherited a College with a rich history and legacy. Firstly, I would like to thank the previous headmasters and in particular John Franklin, the Governing Body and all other stakeholders for the magnificent work they have done for Ardingly.

We are in a position of strength and I am fortunate to take over a school that is full to overflowing (the Shell students have to sit around the steps of the altar); it has also just built a magnificent Pre-Prep whose fabric and quality are designed to last for the next 150 years. It is a sure sign of confidence in our future.

Now we have started a programme of self-review. We are looking at the nature of our admissions, our academic credentials, and our environment, our boarding culture and, not least, our Woodard ethos: what makes us tick? We aim to 'improve on success', building on our academic standing, bettering our environment and restoring the Quadrangles to their original character. Once this piece of work is completed we will be teaching, learning and living in surroundings second to none. As part of this process we have some exciting plans for developing the facilities of the Prep School. It will take time, but such is our confidence in the College that we all believe that this is within reach.

Our vision is to strengthen our Woodard ethos and not lose sight of our mission: we are a co-educational school in the Woodard Corporation founded to teach the Christian faith. Our aim is to enable all boys and girls to develop their love of learning, academic potential and individual talents in a caring community which fosters sensitivity, confidence, a sense of service and enthusiasm for life. We continue to produce young men and women who will go into the world confident in their own faith and being, with a sense of justice for all — along with a desire to make a difference to the wider world as willing recompense for the privileged upbringing they have enjoyed both at home and at College.

Nathaniel Woodard's 'Jewel in the Crown' is looking forward to the next 150 years with confidence and ambition. Our founder had an extraordinary vision, faith and belief in providing a first class education for students. His legacy, as we approach our 150th year at Ardingly, is alive and thriving.

Peter Green, Headmaster.
March 2008

Celebrating the Eucharist in the School Chapel.

Headmaster's Lake.

CHAPTER ONE

The Founder and his Foundation

Stand on the Terrace at Ardingly and admire the stunning view: over the meadows running gently down to the lake, beyond to the low-lying Nine Acre playing fields encircled by the stately River Ouse, across to the steep and wooded hills of River's Wood, and away to the distant arched viaduct carrying the trains of the London—Brighton line. Immediately you appreciate that someone, sometime, had the vision to locate this school so as to create, from landscape and buildings, a magnificent setting.

That someone was Nathaniel Woodard who in 1858 founded St Saviour's School in Shoreham. That time was late in 1861 when, having scoured the south of England for a suitable permanent location for this new school, he came across the 196-acre Saucelands estate, at the southern end of the remote village of Ardingly in the heart of the Sussex Weald. He recognised instinctively that here was a location with potential — an uplifting rural setting well away from the distraction to youth of the city and three miles from Haywards Heath railway station with its access to the London and indeed national market for boarding pupils.

Woodard was a narrow-minded man with a deep Christian faith and a strong sense of purpose. Appreciating the lack of good schools for the newly emerged middle classes, he set out to build a national network of Anglican schools which would also enable the established church, the Church of England, to recapture the heart and soul of the nation. Ardingly, with fees of no more than £15 per annum, was created specifically for the 'sons of small shopkeepers, farmers, mechanics and others of limited means', collectively the lower middle classes. He regarded it as the very heart of his grand design.

Nathaniel Woodard was born in 1811 at Basildon in Essex, the son of an impoverished gentleman, the ninth of a family of twelve children. We know little about his childhood and upbringing. What education he had was limited to tuition in private homes, and there is certainly no evidence that he went to a formal school. Fortuitously the financial support of two aunts enabled him to go up to Magdalen Hall (now Hertford College), Oxford in 1834, where he resided on and off for six years before taking a pass degree in 1840. It was there that he became deeply influenced by the Oxford Movement, that influential body of opinion which rejected the

The Reverend Nathaniel Woodard (1811–91), the School's founder.

Protestant element in Anglicanism in favour of the Catholic as it existed before the Reformation and which denied the rights of Parliament to oversee the affairs of the Church. Most unusually for an undergraduate, he had married in 1836.

Following graduation, he was ordained in 1841 by Bishop Blomfield of London into a curacy at a newly built church, St Bartholomew's, Bethnal Green, then as now one of the poorest and most transient parts of the capital. Two years later however he was removed from his post by the Bishop following a sermon in which he was alleged to have advocated auricular confession. Confession was seen by the Anglican Church as a Papist characteristic. It was approved by Anglicans only for the sick and the dying. Woodard's apparent advocacy of confession, allied to his inability and/or unwillingness to assuage

The original house which together with its estate was purchased by Woodard in 1862.

The contract to buy the estate, signed by Woodard.

the turning point in his life's work. His parishioners were local tradesmen, clerks, a smattering of farmers and sea captains, many of them engaged in the trade of the port — coal from the Tyne, timber, grain and other goods to and from the Baltic. He was surprised by their lack of education and that many were in fact illiterate. It was not long therefore before he had established a simple school in his drawing room for the local children. It was a success and soon he had expanded out of his house and was attracting resident pupils from further afield.

Woodard's life spanned most of the 19th century, a period during which Britain grew not only in numbers (18 million in 1811 at his birth, 38 million in 1891 when he died) but also in wealth and prosperity. The new industrial and urban Britain was rapidly replacing an agricultural economy and rural society, and playing a key role in this transformation were the fast emerging middle classes. Here was what was to become the backbone of a modern industrial society — the lawyers, doctors, teachers, farmers, engineers, tradesmen, shopkeepers, clerks and administrators — which ever since has been referred to as Middle England.

his critics, were to dog his career throughout. He was lucky indeed to be given a second chance in a curacy in Hackney.

In 1846, perhaps to get this marked man out of the way, Woodard was moved to a curacy at Shoreham in Sussex. He was put in charge of New Shoreham, the busiest part of the parish, by the harbour at the mouth of the River Adur and six miles west of the rapidly growing Brighton. This was to be

In 1846, Woodard moved to Shoreham and set up a simple school in his house (shown here). Two years later he founded the New Shoreham Grammar School.

NEW SHOREHAM GRAMMAR SCHOOL.

The Inhabitants of Shoreham and the neighbourhood have now an opportunity of giving their children, (at a very small charge per quarter), a Religious, and good sound commercial Education, together with the elements of Latin and French.

At present a form is assigned them at the upper part of the Boys' Parochial School, but ultimately, a building will, by God's blessing, be procured.

Boys above the age of six years, will receive instruction in the usual branches of an English education, including, Book-keeping, Navigation, Land Surveying, Mensuration, &c., &c.; to which will be added the elements of Latin and French.

TERMS :—To Parishioners .. .. £1 0 0 Per Quarter.
,, Without Latin and French .. 0 15 0 ,,

RULES AND REGULATIONS.

1.—Each Boy will be expected to attend the daily morning prayers at Church, unless he obtain leave of absence from the Head master ; and those Boys who live in the parish of New Shoreham must attend on Sundays.

2.—School-hours, for the present, from Nine to Twelve A.M. and from Two to Five P.M. Wednesdays and Saturdays half-holidays.

3.—Marks of Merit will be registered, which will be assigned for the following acts — Regular and punctual attendance at School and Prayers—General good and respectful conduct in School—Lessons accurately learnt and Books cleanly and neatly kept—Diligent application and Religious habits.

4.—Twice a year (at Christmas and Midsummer,) there will be a public examination of the children by some Clergyman unconnected with the parish, who will have the "Mark Register" and his own observation, to guide him in awarding the prizes.

5.—At the first public examination after the school has been in operation one year, a prize of £10 will be given to the best boy as an apprenticeship premium. In case the boy to whom the prize is assigned is too young to leave home, the money will be invested in the Savings' bank for him, and paid over to him with the accumulations on his apprenticeship. Other sums varying according to merit, will be given to the *three* next best boys and invested in the Savings' bank for their use, no boy eligible to stand for these prizes who has not been on the books one year.

6.—Prizes of useful and religious books will be awarded according to the deserts of the pupils, in determining which, a conscientious discharge of the duties of the school and good religious habits will be more regarded than intellectual qualities.

7.—At each public examination, the best boy in the parochial school will be elected into the grammar school, where he will receive his education free of expence, and be eligible to the grammar school prizes.

8.—The internal rules and regulations of the school, will be framed by the clergy of the parish, and will be acted upon without any deviation.

9.—Bills to be paid quarterly, there will be no extras except school books.

10.—A quarter's notice must be given before removing a boy from school.

Application for admission to be made either to

The Rev. W. Wheeler, Vicar, at the Vicarage, Old Shoreham ; or
The Rev. N. Woodard, Curate of New Shoreham, at the Vicarage.

But the 1840s, the decade in which Woodard was launching his great work, was also a period of turbulence in society and politics. Overpopulation, high food prices, famine in Ireland, urban squalor and disease culminated in what became known as the 'Hungry Forties'. Class divisions were exacerbated. This led to agitation that resulted in the repeal of the Corn Laws in 1846 and saw the Chartist movement rising to its peak with the immense Kennington Common demonstration of 1848. Characteristically, though Britain avoided significant upheaval in this year, Europe was to know it simply as the Year of Revolutions. The Red Flag flew in Paris and Karl Marx published his *Communist Manifesto*. It was Woodard's clear belief that these disconcerting events were the product of a secular society and, in particular, secular education.

Woodard recognised that the educational system as a whole failed to provide for the sons of the middle classes. The parochial schools gave a limited elementary education to the working classes. The public schools, stimulated and publicised by Dr Arnold at Rugby, and with new foundations in the 1840s such as Cheltenham, Marlborough and Radley, catered for the upper classes. The middle classes found the parochial schools limited and could not afford the public schools. Furthermore, they regarded the classical curriculum of the moribund grammar schools as irrelevant to their needs. Woodard had seen at first hand, both in London's East End and in Shoreham, that there was no worthwhile education for the sons of tradesmen, farmers and clerks.

Religion drove his work. Believing in the need to place the established church at the heart of national life, he saw education as the means by which the Church of England could resist the challenge of the state and the Nonconformists.

Eighteen forty-eight was to be a crucial year in his great educational plan. First he founded New Shoreham Grammar School as the starting point of his national project, with its own separate buildings adjacent to the church of St Mary de Haura, New Shoreham, and second he published what was to be his manifesto, *A Plea For The Middle Classes*. The aim was 'the provision of a good and complete education for the middle classes, at such a charge as will make it available for most of them'. But this

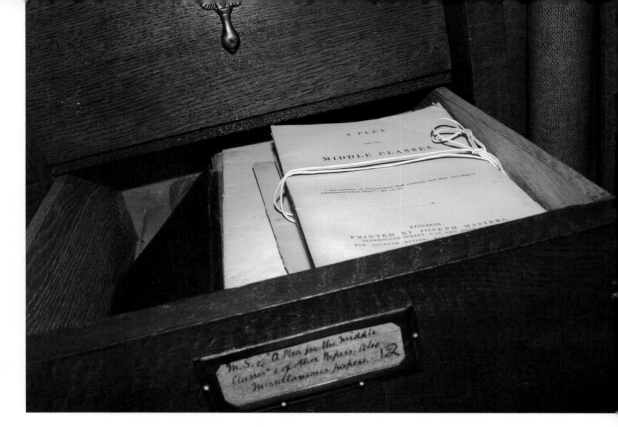

Woodard published his manifesto A Plea For The Middle Classes *in 1848 in which he outlined his plan to offer a 'good and complete education' for the middle classes at affordable prices.*

was to be no ordinary education: *'It is my earnest wish, and the object and intention of all the Benefactors, that for all future time the sons of any of Her then Majesty's subjects should be taught, together with sound grammar learning, the fear and honour of Almighty God, the Father, Son and the Holy Ghost, according to the doctrines of the Catholic Faith as it is now set forth in the Book of the Offices and Administration of the Sacraments of the Church of England.'* And soon afterwards, so as to have a vehicle to make it all happen, he founded the Society of St Nicolas (now known as the Woodard Corporation). It was to be governed by a Provost (himself at the outset) and sixteen Fellows.

Woodard was a product of the Victorian age. He thought in terms of structures and systems, and he saw society in terms of class. It is not surprising therefore that his scheme for a national group of schools for the middle classes had three distinct tiers or grades:

The Upper or First Tier Schools were for the sons of gentlemen, officers, clergymen and superior trades people. The fees were to be £30 per annum and it was hoped that these schools would provide both funds and teachers for the two lower tier schools. Shoreham Grammar School, founded as we have seen in 1848, was designated as the first upper tier school and it developed into Lancing College, moving to its permanent home in 1858.

The Middle or Second Tier Schools were for the sons of tradesmen, farmers and superior clerks and charged 18 guineas per annum. The first of this kind was opened as St John's at New Shoreham in 1849 and transferred to Hurstpierpoint when its buildings there were completed in 1853.

The Lower Middle or Third Tier Schools were for the sons of small shopkeepers, mechanics, clerks and others of limited means and charged fees of £15 per annum. It was expected that no parent would have an income in excess of £150 per annum. The first of these third tier schools was called St Saviour's School and was founded in the New Shoreham buildings vacated by Lancing on 12th April 1858. It was transplanted to its permanent home at Ardingly in 1870. It is this community which is the subject of this book.

The first grade schools were to act as centres for groups of associated second and third grade schools, with a Provost residing at each centre. The plan was for a series of such groups, or divisions as they became known in due course, throughout the land.

But what every schoolteacher knows is that to label any school or pupil as third class becomes a self-fulfilling reality. No matter how virtuous the motive, Ardingly was stuck very much at the bottom of the pile. There was however to be a ladder of opportunity, enabling the brightest boys to be able to gain scholarships to move up from the lower middle to

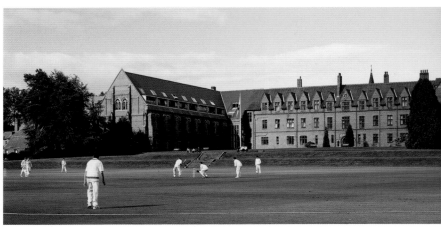

Denstone College and Ellesmere College – both fine examples of Woodard's vision for his schools with their majestic chapels and imposing Gothic architecture.

middle and ultimately upper tier schools. Thus in contemporary egalitarian-speak, there existed the chance for a young boy of talent from a disadvantaged background to work his way up to the upper tier school and then ultimately to Oxford or Cambridge.

To enable fees to be kept at such low levels, it was necessary to minimise costs. Teachers, the most important single component in any school, are expensive. Woodard wanted all his heads and most of his teachers to be in Holy Orders. Some came on very low stipends, seeing their vocation in doing God's work. He developed the concept of 'monitors', senior pupils who for a very low fee received some teaching and also taught the younger pupils. He also established at Hurstpierpoint in 1853 what was, in effect, a training college for teachers, whereby so-called 'probationers' learned on the job, hoping to gain a teaching qualification by becoming what the Founder designated as an Associate of the Society of St Nicolas.

His plans for education were not confined solely to schools. In 1850 he helped to found the Leyton Military and Engineering College, providing a technical and vocational training in this densely populated area on the edge of the East End of London. It never really became established and closed down in 1857. Likewise his plans to create halls of residence for the products of his schools at Oxford and Cambridge at much cheaper rates than conventional college life, in the end came to nothing.

He designed this network of schools for the middle classes as a means of doing the Church of England's work. Majestic chapels, Gothic architecture and plainsong music were distinguishing characteristics of what had become known as the Anglo-Catholic strand of the Church of England. Woodard's schools became epitomes of this tradition.

In 1849 Woodard resigned his curacy in Shoreham so that he could devote the whole of his time and energies to the Society of St Nicolas. The pace was relentless. First to be built was Hurstpierpoint (1850–53), next Lancing (1854–58), and then, established in the buildings vacated by Lancing at New Shoreham, St Saviour's was founded in 1858. There it remained for 12 years until it transferred to its new site at Ardingly, constructed spasmodically and incompletely between 1864 and 1870.

As Provost of the Society, Woodard was a one-man governing body of each of the schools. Autocratic, energetic, unceasing in his endeavours, he did everything. Between 1849 and 1860 he raised just over £100,000 (approximately £5m in today's terms). Now we would regard him as a single-minded and formidably determined school development officer. He wrote numerous fundraising pamphlets and individual letters. Public occasions, such as a formal opening, were an opportunity for a splendid luncheon to which the great, the good and the well-heeled were invited. On each plate was a subscription form. No one left without having handed it in. Those who did not immediately subscribe were followed up methodically. Collections of £500 at services on special occasions were not unknown. Fundraising committees were established in Oxford, Cambridge, London and Brighton.

Woodard became an accomplished fund raiser, holding meetings across the country to publicise his planned network of schools. Martin Gibbs (right), was an enthusiastic supporter who gave generously to both Lancing and Ardingly.

Woodard was well connected. From his days in Oxford and in the East End of London, he had come to know many of the leading High Churchmen, lay and clerical, of the day. Although austere and without obvious social charm, he was a persuasive man who somehow managed to win their confidence. William Gladstone and the Marquess of Salisbury, both future prime ministers, were prepared to chair meetings on behalf of the Society; bankers such as Henry Tritton of Barclay, Bevan & Tritton and William Cotton of the Bank of England, gave generously; so too did Martin Gibbs, wealthy philanthropist, and A.J. Beresford Hope, MP and founder of the Camden Society for Church Buildings; other supporters were the Baltic merchant, J.E. Hubbard (later Lord Addington) and Sir John Patteson, the Exchequer Court judge.

We know from our own age that religion has the capacity both to unite and to divide. Symbols can be misinterpreted and a group of schools espousing one particular brand of the Christian faith was seen as a threat by some. The meeting held in Brighton in 1856 and chaired by Gladstone aroused fierce criticism in the local press on grounds of religious bigotry. And then in 1861 at Oxford, long a strong source of financial support, Dr Golightly, Fellow of Oriel, launched an assault, which included handing out leaflets as the 2,000 guests filed into the Sheldonian Theatre, claiming that 'confession is encouraged among the boys' and 'crucifixes are distributed among the boys leaving the School'.

Woodard was not good at defending himself. For all his marketing and missionary zeal, he had no feel for what we now call 'public relations'. He was never a commanding public speaker and perhaps he was over-confident of his position but he refused to make a statement categorically denying the allegations. No matter the facts of the situation, for many years it was widely believed that confession was practised in Woodard's schools and this led to the drying up of support from Oxford.

Eighteen seventy marked the midway point in the evolution of the Society of St Nicolas. It was in this year that St Saviour's moved from its original home in Shoreham to Ardingly in the heart of the Sussex Weald. The three tier system was now firmly established in Sussex and Woodard felt able therefore to shift his focus to the Midlands and later to the West Country. He, too, moved his base to Manchester where Prime Minister Gladstone had granted him a canonry at the cathedral. Denstone, a middle tier school (the equivalent of Hurstpierpoint) opened in Staffordshire in 1873; Ellesmere, a lower middle (like Ardingly) in Shropshire in 1884; and King's College, Taunton, was a refoundation in 1880 as the Society moved westwards.

From 1870, however, the soil for Woodard's schools became more stony and less fertile, as the state began to plug the gap and provide schooling for the nation as a whole. The Endowed Schools Act of

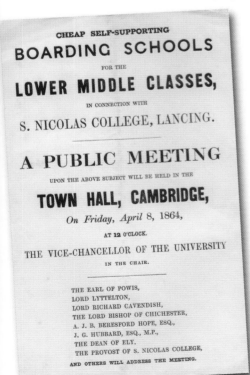

A poster advertising one of many public meetings organised by Woodard to set out his educational vision and to raise funds.

The magnificent Gothic chapel of Lancing College, on the edge of the Sussex Downs.

1869, which followed up the Schools Enquiry of 1865, was important in the wider scheme of things. The Tudor and Stuart grammar school foundations had been moribund for a long time. Founded by wealthy merchants, often in their home town (for example Sir Andrew Judde in Tonbridge in 1553) or by churchmen (for example Archbishop Samuel Harsnett in Chigwell in 1629), they had been designed to give a sound education for the local people in the ancient languages Latin and Greek, the former of course being the language of government and court, often in a Protestant environment. Their statutes were remarkably similar and proved to be very restrictive, for example limiting the salaries of the Master and Usher (the senior teacher) to a fixed sum. By the 19th century most of them were dormant, especially after the Eldon Judgement of 1805 which confirmed that only the ancient languages could be taught. Now, however, the Act of 1869 enabled their statutes to be redrawn. Many of them therefore were refounded, brought into the modern world with a modern curriculum and, aided by railways and urban growth, offered a very acceptable education to local communities. The need for new boarding schools for the middle classes became less apparent.

And to some extent also, enthusiasm for Woodard's schools died with the collapse of opposition. Dr Golightly had gone away and the fear of Papist tendencies had disappeared. Nothing brings together an organisation, especially in a religious context, like the feeling of persecution. Acceptance often brings complacency.

The 1880s found Woodard tired. Ardingly, as we shall see, lacked the most basic facilities and was desperately under funded but he spent most of his time and diminishing energies endeavouring to build the Lancing Chapel as the central minster of the Society. This bottomless pit significantly weakened the whole organisation and, in particular, Ardingly. Woodard, as Provost, dominated the Society he had founded, and which paid him a substantial salary between 1849 and 1870. He was not checked by the Fellows. A lack of appropriate financial and administrative management meant that Ardingly suffered.

Woodard died in 1891. About his private life we know little. His sons went to Lancing and one of them, Billy, as we shall see, worked for many years at Ardingly in the role of Clerk of Works. Woodard's wife died in the 1870s and remarkably, aged 80, he was married again to a lady of 23, the daughter of a schoolmaster. Tantalisingly, we know little about this marriage and only a year later, in 1891, he died. There are some 9,000 letters written by and to him in the Woodard Archive at Lancing College but they deal without exception with the Society of St Nicolas. There is no hint in this correspondence of any broader life,

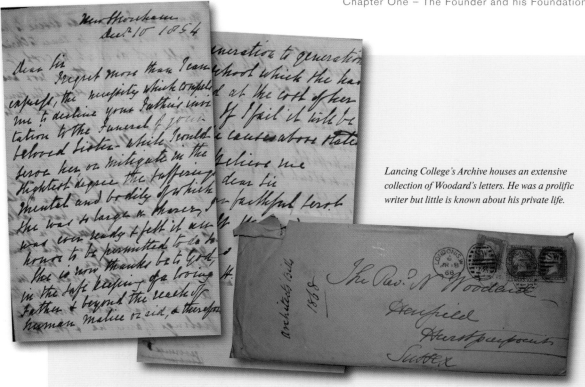

Lancing College's Archive houses an extensive collection of Woodard's letters. He was a prolific writer but little is known about his private life.

any knowledge of his interests or passions, no evidence of a wider hinterland. He had no real philosophy of education, unlike Cardinal Newman, and he was not a reformer, unlike Thomas Arnold. He showed no recognition or knowledge of the work of Edward Thring at Uppingham or F.W. Sanderson at Oundle, both of whom set out creatively to modernise the curriculum with not only science but also art and design. Woodard's achievements were essentially in bricks and mortar and in the Holy Spirit. By the time of his death, he had founded no fewer than nine schools himself and a further three had joined his scheme. While this fell short of his vision of a national system of Church of England boarding schools, he

had nevertheless established the most extensive educational organisation in England that has endured and expanded to 35 schools today. And what is more, the Woodard Corporation is currently involved in planning for the establishment of three City Academies in that triangle of West Sussex embracing Lancing, Shoreham and Littlehampton, going right back to its roots, in meeting the needs of the nation, albeit this time in partnership with the state.

The Founder of Ardingly was laid to rest in medieval state in his own chantry in the great central minster of his Society at Lancing looking down on the poor and humble port community of Shoreham where it had all begun.

Woodard's tomb in his beloved Lancing College Chapel.

Bluebells along the Cinder path in Kiln Wood.

CHAPTER TWO

Mertens and Shoreham Days 1858–70

St Saviour's School opened its doors on 12th April 1858. It occupied the buildings in the lee of the churchyard of St Mary de Haura recently vacated by the boys of Shoreham Grammar School, which had become Lancing College and now moved to its own permanent premises conspicuously located across the valley high on the edge of the Downs. Five years earlier, in 1853, Hurstpierpoint College had moved from the same Shoreham origins to be established in a small village at the foot of the scarp slope of the Downs, eight miles north of Brighton. Now was the opportunity for the seed of the third tier school to be sown and then, when conditions were ripe, to be transplanted to an appropriate permanent home. It was to prove a long 12-year wait till that moment arrived, with St Saviour's finally moving to Ardingly in 1870.

To the vital position of Headmaster, Woodard appointed Revd Frederick Mertens, a graduate of St John's College, Oxford, and previously on the staff of Shoreham Grammar School. Mertens was to give his life's work to this community and, when he retired 36 years later, Ardingly College was firmly established as a major institution in the Sussex landscape. He had launched the School from scratch

The Reverend Frederick Mertens, the first headmaster of St Saviour's in Shoreham, held his post from 1858-94. The School moved to Ardingly in 1870.

in its homely cluster of cramped buildings in Shoreham, overseen the difficult and long-delayed move to an unfinished site at Ardingly, and then ensured over the next quarter of a century that it was much more than simply a third grade school.

We get a good picture of life at Shoreham from a series of articles written more than 40 years later in 1912–14 for the School magazine, the *Ardingly Annals*, by three former pupils, C.M. Neale, C.E. Scholes and W.J. Downer.

Able, kindly and humorous, Mertens, the Headmaster, was a popular figure amongst the boys. They sensed instinctively his broadminded nature and essential fairness, respected his marked capabilities and admired his public performances in Chapel and on High Days and Holy Days. They loved his occasional spoonerisms, whether deliberate or not, for example that recorded by Neale: '... it is easier for a camel to go through the knee of an idol'. His intelligent management of people and limited resources, together with his huge commitment to the cause and stoicism in the face of innumerable difficulties, were crucial in the creation and establishment of Ardingly.

For that first summer at Shoreham in 1858, there were nine pupils. A year later there were 100, and by 1866 numbers had grown to 309. St Saviour's was an immediate success. Of course, the very low fees at £15 per annum helped. And parents did everything they could to qualify for entry for their sons by showing that their income was less than the

The Main School building at Shoreham.

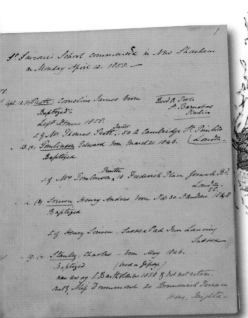

Opening page of the School register, 1858.

£150 per annum maximum set by Woodard for his third tier schools. The downside of the low fees, however, was that conditions were basic. The dormitories were extremely cramped, the teaching facilities limited and the food too often inadequate.

The key factor in keeping fees so low was the very low staffing costs. Mertens' salary as Headmaster had started at £100 per annum and risen to £200 per annum (plus a capitation fee of £114) by 1869 (by comparison, the Master of Wellington College, responsible for roughly the same number of pupils, was earning just over £2,000 per annum at this time). The Chaplain and Senior Master (Revd F.K. Hilton throughout the Shoreham period) each earned £75 per annum and a junior master less than £50. Excepting the Headmaster, the staff were all single men living in essence a monastic life in undertaking, as they saw it, God's work. Some were recent graduates who gave their service voluntarily, in the same way that people today are persuaded to go abroad to teach in Africa on Voluntary Service Overseas. St Saviour's also made much use of probationers, who were unqualified teachers, many of them old boys of Lancing, hoping to gain the qualification of Associate of the Society of St Nicolas by learning on the job. As well there were 'servitors'

who paid a reduced fee of £5 pa and were given three hours' education in the afternoons in return for undertaking domestic duties in the mornings.

The pupils lived in a cluster of buildings in Church Street, adjacent to the parish church and running down to the River Adur. The main school building had several teaching rooms and a second-floor chapel. Opened in 1860, its funding had been aided by Magdalen College, Oxford, High Church in flavour, and in whose gift the living of the parish lay. The Head's House (No.22 Church Street) had resident pupils, School House (No.24) had two large dormitories, and more pupils lived at Mr Harris's House (No.15).

The aim of the third tier schools, as Woodard had decreed, was to prepare boys for a business life, not for university and the professions, and so the curriculum at St Saviour's was necessarily limited to mathematics, basic literature, and a little Latin and French. Most pupils would leave at 14 or 16, and although those who did show promise could win scholarships to Hurstpierpoint or even Lancing, few in practice did so.

Given the need to keep staffing costs low, the quality of the teaching, and what would now be called pastoral care, must have varied considerably, as suggested by these former pupils.

Frederick Mertens with his wife and children. He is thought to have had 13 children.

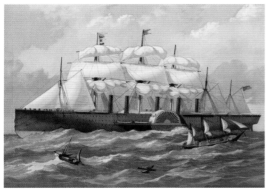

Brunel's Great Eastern *steam ship was launched in 1858. One Shoreham pupil recalled how he and his friends gaped in awe as the world's biggest ship sailed gracefully by.*

Scholes: *'The masters I remember were Mr Caporn, the Chaplain, Mr Fuller, afterwards Chaplain, Osmond Cookson, my ideal, Mr Woodward (nicknamed Phummee) a spiteful man who caned James until his back was a terrible state of weals.'*

Downer: *'Mr Harris was very human and one liked him, he was our librarian, stationer and came into familiar touch with every boy. Mr Cookson came towards the end of my time. He was of quite a different stamp from any other master, a muscular Christian, with short, dark, curly hair; he was very friendly and a good all-round sportsman. I was very fond of him.'*

And Neale: *'The Rev. Osmond Cookson was not the Chaplain but was conspicuous for his physical strength and his sermons. These were extraordinarily popular, preached extempore and usually less than a quarter of an hour. A later Chaplain, the Rev. Ormsby Handcock, was regarded as a marvel of erudition. He was a very kind man, but his personal appearance did not favour him. He was tall and thin, wore an untrimmed beard and had a slight awkwardness of manner ... his sermons lasted from forty-five to fifty-five minutes; our enjoyment may be imagined ... He left us in 1870 to take up missionary work in East Africa but died in Zanzibar that September.'*

Games were played on the flat ground by the side of the harbour, known locally as the Hard, and starting in 1859 a limited amount of cricket and football was played on a rough field outside the town. The name, Hard, familiar to every Ardinian, came with the School when it moved to its permanent home, and is the playing field immediately on the right-hand side after passing through the gates. Athletic sports were always contested in the autumn. Swimming in the sea was obviously a summer activity and involved crossing the toll bridge and then a mile-long walk to the isolated and desolate beach, nowadays crowded with bungalows. One day, Neale recorded he and his friends gaping with awe as

On a school trip to Brighton in the 1860s pupils saw Blondin, the French tightrope walker, famous for traversing the gorge at Niagara Falls. Known for his stunts, he once carried a stove across the gorge, stopped half way across and cooked an omelette. He is shown here crossing with his manager on his back.

At Shoreham sport was played on the 'Hard', an area of land by the harbour. The name stuck and moved with the school to Ardingly.

Brunel's *Great Eastern*, then the biggest ship in the world, sailed gracefully by. The bicycle had not yet been invented but the open Downs a mile from the settlement of Shoreham were a wonderful natural playground for long walks, paper chase runs and picnics. Occasional special visits to Brighton were long remembered, not least trips to the Swiss Gardens for concerts and fireworks and on one memorable occasion to see Blondin the famous tightrope walker.

A carving of St Nicolas at Lancing College.

Activities were not only physical. Neale records hugely enjoyable plays in the dining hall, as well as the delights of the library, discovering those characteristic Victorian stories for schoolboys by Captain Marryat and Mr Ballantyne, and, of course, Dickens.

The Chapel above the main schoolroom could only accommodate half the School, and so one half of the pupils attended in the morning and the other half in the evening. On Sundays the School provided the choir in St Mary de Haura, the parish church adjacent to the School, and a small group of pupils led the singing at the small church at Old Shoreham at the other end of the parish. But there was no hothouse religious atmosphere as Woodard's critics contended, and the tone and nature of the services were generally acceptable to all branches of the Christian faith.

The long hours of schooling seem excessively harsh to us in the early 21st century, but it needs to be remembered that these were the norm at this time. On weekdays the rising bell was at 6.30am and most would not get to bed till 9.30pm. Scholes reports two slices of bread and butter plus a mug of water or milk for breakfast and then a substantial midday meal. The school year was long. It was divided into two halves, the first from the end of January to the end of June, the second from the end of July to the week before Christmas. There were regular holidays, though – All Saints and Ascension Day, St Nicolas' Day (6th December) and for special occasions such as the marriage of the Prince of Wales (later Edward VII) to Princess Alexandra of Denmark in 1863.

St Mary de Haura in New Shoreham.

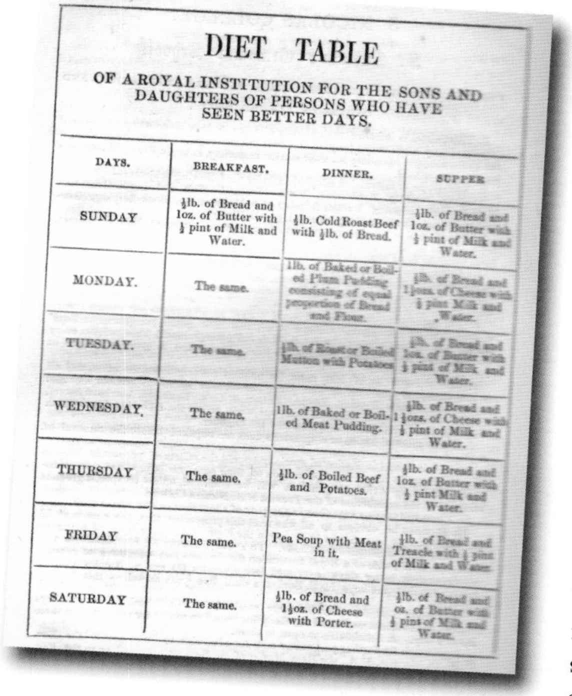

DIET TABLE

OF A ROYAL INSTITUTION FOR THE SONS AND DAUGHTERS OF PERSONS WHO HAVE SEEN BETTER DAYS.

DAYS.	BREAKFAST.	DINNER.	SUPPER
SUNDAY	½lb. of Bread and 1oz. of Butter with ½ pint of Milk and Water.	¼lb. Cold Roast Beef with ¼lb. of Bread.	¼lb. of Bread and 1oz. of Butter with ½ pint of Milk and Water.
MONDAY.	The same.	1lb. of Baked or Boiled Plum Pudding consisting of equal proportion of Bread and Flour.	¼lb. of Bread and 1½ozs. of Cheese with ½ pint Milk and Water.
TUESDAY.	The same.	¼lb. of Roast or Boiled Mutton with Potatoes.	¼lb. of Bread and 1oz. of Butter with ½ pint of Milk and Water.
WEDNESDAY.	The same.	1lb. of Baked or Boiled Meat Pudding.	¼lb. of Bread and 1½ozs. of Cheese with ½ pint of Milk and Water.
THURSDAY	The same.	½lb. of Boiled Beef and Potatoes.	¼lb. of Bread and 1oz. of Butter with ½ pint Milk and Water.
FRIDAY	The same.	Pea Soup with Meat in it.	¼lb. of Bread and Treacle with ½ pint of Milk and Water.
SATURDAY	The same.	¼lb. of Bread and 1½oz. of Cheese with Porter.	¼lb. of Bread and oz. of Butter with ½ pint of Milk and Water.

A recommended diet from 1861 found in the School's archives.

Victorian boarding school life could be brutal and harsh. Riots were not unknown. George McDonald Fraser's Flashman at Rugby may have been fictitious but such bullying characters were all too frequent in the memoirs of former pupils. For a variety of reasons the worst excesses of boarding school life were avoided at St Saviour's. Most of the pupils came from families who had little formal education, and so there was therefore no family tradition of boarding with its bullying and unpleasantness. The School buildings were small and homely, the atmosphere essentially friendly. A true Christian philosophy did pervade. An ethos of fundamental decency was created, which was transferred to Ardingly and has survived ever since.

Although Woodard himself appeared occasionally for the main religious festivals, his body and mind were essentially elsewhere. On resigning his curacy in 1849 to take up the full-time work of building his national network of schools, he had moved from the vicarage at New Shoreham seven miles away to Henfield. Mertens was left to get on with the business of creating and directing the School. The lack of interference by the Founder was a distinct advantage; the lack of progress on locating and then constructing the School's permanent home was not.

The Shoreham site was never considered more than a makeshift residence. Short-term privations could be borne in the anticipation of more comforts and buildings better adapted for a school. Out of sight, out of mind, Woodard was trying to complete his work at Lancing and the raising of funds was proving difficult.

It was not until 1862 that a suitable site for the third tier school was acquired, and then in 1863 Woodard on one of his occasional visits to the School told the boys with great enthusiasm and excitement about the new buildings which were about to go up. With typical Woodardian ceremony the foundation stone for St Saviour's School at Ardingly was laid on 12th July 1864 but it was to be another six years before the move was actually undertaken.

The community at New Shoreham was warm, friendly and homely. Few would claim that the education provided was first-class and nor was it modern. It did not pretend to prepare boys for university and the professions. It was however a firmly established, successful and virile community that was now to be transplanted, and it did provide a basic training and start in life for a wide range of young people. It was also remarkably healthy, despite the crowding. The bracing sea air and plenty of physical activity outside the bustling village helped in this, as too did the school doctor, who according to Hilton had two remedies only: half a tumbler of cough mixture or the extraction of a tooth!

The foundation stone for the School at Ardingly.

North Quad at night.

CHAPTER THREE

The Move to Ardingly 1870

The school for the sons of those of limited means was the real heart of Woodard's scheme. Yet during the early 1850s, he was preoccupied with establishing the first and second tier schools, Lancing and Hurstpierpoint, and so the planning, and especially the financing of the third tier, was largely ignored. Ardingly was to have a far more difficult start than either of its two ostensibly superior cousins: in fact it was markedly neglected.

A pamphlet of 1854 did eventually set out the aim – a site of at least 150 acres, 20–30 miles from London, and for a massive 1,000 pupils. These would be divided into three separate parts with three individual heads, two roughly comparable senior schools and one junior, yet sharing key facilities such as catering, a chapel and games fields. Woodard's grasp of fundamental school economics was sound: the principle of economies of scale is enduring. Schools, however, are not factories and the last 40 years has shown that very large schools tend to fail. There is an optimum size for a school community, big enough to share basic costs, small enough so that pupils can feel they belong and are known. In fact, fortuitously, the 1,000 strong Ardingly was never remotely achieved.

Attempts at fundraising were less successful. The conventional meetings in Oxford and Cambridge were held, though as we have seen the attacks led by Dr Golightly with their accusations of auricular confession were harmful. Woodard did not defend his corner well and an opportunity was missed. Committees were established in both London and Brighton which did enable the project to get under way, but it was to be nearly 100 years before the School's finances could be considered even remotely sound.

Eventually the estate at Ardingly was acquired for £6,000. Saucelands, a Tudor ironmaster's house together with its woodland, steep gullies with fast-flowing streams, and fields of oats and hops was 30 miles from the middle of London. Set on a hillside, just to the south of the village, it looked down to the valley of the River Ouse and across to the magnificent viaduct carrying the London, Brighton and South Coast Railway north to London, south to Haywards Heath and Brighton. Apart from the occasional farm building, this was the only sign of human settlement. The Victorian public school

Great Saucelands – Ardingly

builders sought such sites well away from the temptations of town and city.

Ardingly is an Anglo-Saxon name meaning the clearing (ly) of the people of Earda or Eored, laboriously cut out of the great forest known as the Weald, or, as the Romans called it, Anderida. Remote and unpopulated, it had never been a manor in its own right. The people of the prosperous villages at the foot of the scarp slope of the Downs – South Malling, Ditchling, Streat and Plumpton – had used the land for grazing their pigs, an early example of transhumance. The advent of the Wakehurst family (Wakehurst Place is now in the hands of the National Trust and well known as the outpost of the Royal Botanic Gardens at Kew) in the 13th century created some prosperity. So, too, did the Wealden iron industry in the 16th century – a furnace at Stroudgate, a forge at Fulling Mill, the Bloomer Valley at Wakehurst.

Ardinians who have played their games on Nine Acre will be surprised to know that during the period

The purchase of the Saucelands Estate in 1862 was the first step in moving the School from Shoreham to Ardingly.

The magnificent Ouse viaduct, opened in 1841.

of the Industrial Revolution barges briefly used the River Ouse, following the building of locks and cuts to make it navigable from its mouth at Newhaven to Balcombe Wharf, where now stands the railway viaduct. The Upper Ouse Navigation Company never paid a dividend but it did help to open up this remote part of rural Sussex.

Even so the 1861 census recorded a mere 658 people living in the village of Ardingly. It was a relatively poor community, with most of the inhabitants employed in agriculture, primarily as labourers. There was however a village school, charging 2d per week for a child, with 1d for each additional sibling. The elementary education provided was basic and although its aims — 'The object of this school is to train children to fear God, to obey their parents, and to live according to the Faith in Christ as true members of His Body, the Church' — would have appealed to Woodard, he had bigger fish to fry.

*A pamphlet outlining Woodard's ambitious plans for his
'Lower Middle' School at Ardingly, Sussex.*

Remote and with uplifting views, Ardingly also possessed, albeit at some distance, the other prerequisite for a Victorian public school, a railway. The London to Brighton line had been built between 1838 and 1841 and included the spectacular viaduct across the Ouse Valley, a mile from the School. But the nearest station was three miles away in Haywards Heath, a simple journey by horse-drawn cab or a lengthy walk up and down hill.

After the abortive attempts to build the Ouse Valley line in 1864–66 (a branch line from Haywards Heath to Uckfield via the Ouse Valley which was never completed although surviving earthworks can still be seen), Ardingly had to wait until 1883 when the East Grinstead railway opened its own station half a mile down the road, as the *Mid-Sussex Times* reported: '... not only a useful adjunct of Ardingly Village, but an architectural ornament to this neighbourhood ... The Ardingly rustics, no more than

the Collegians, will have cause to be proud of their little railway station.' It was to play an essential and intimate part in the life of every Ardinian till it closed 80 years later in 1963.

The architect, as with all Woodard's Sussex schools, was R.H. Carpenter. The style was Early Pointed with cusped windows in the wings and traceried windows elsewhere. The red facing bricks were made on site in Kiln Wood, whilst the stone came from a quarry at Scaynes Hill. The foundation stone was laid with much ceremony on 12th July

The School engine at Ardingly Station. The Station, open from 1883–1963, was used by generations of Ardinians.

View of the School taken from Headmaster's Lake.

*Drawings published in The Builder showing plans for
the School at Ardingly, 1867.*

Left: The contract with the builders signed by Woodard.

the Founder, became in effect the Clerk of Works and was to remain at Ardingly for most of the rest of his life.

Work continued spasmodically. Parties of boys and masters who came over from Shoreham to see how the work was progressing often found nothing was happening. Eventually, however, perhaps in something of a triumph of hope over experience, it was decided to move the School to its new home.

On 14th June 1870 the 250 boys of St Saviour's rose at dawn, took Communion at 5.45am and then set off by train for Haywards Heath. They walked the three miles to the College on a hot summer's day, attended a variety of festivities, including the formal dedication ceremony, and then returned by the same means to Shoreham for one final day before breaking up for their summer holiday.

The warmth, snugness and cosiness of Shoreham life was to be left behind in exchange for a rudimentary shell of buildings on an exposed hill on the edge of woods.

1864 and, as so often, Woodard had assembled a formidable team led by the Lord President of the Council, Earl Granville, to conduct the formalities. The building programme was however anything but straightforward. The contractor was not paid and had to go to court to be reimbursed. Billy Woodard, son of

The Chapel and Tower.

CHAPTER FOUR

Establishing the School at Ardingly 1870–94

On 28th July 1870, 280 boys arrived at Ardingly. The School, as they had seen in June, was not ready. Three blocks had been completed externally — Headmaster's House, School House and the Dining Hall block. There was however no heating or lighting, and in Headmaster's House there was no running water. The foundations of the Chapel had been laid but there was no connecting path or passage between Headmaster's House and the Dining Hall and School House. Of North School, there was no sign. There were, of course, no checks in the form of building regulations and inspectors, but to move the School in such conditions was a considerable act of faith. And there was no great prospect of anything much happening in the near future as the School's unpaid debts of £4,000 were already a huge burden.

The sanitary conditions were extremely primitive and soon they were to take their toll. Scarlet fever broke out and between 22nd August and 19th September five boys died. Death rates were, of course, higher then than they are now. Disease in Victorian England was ever present, and in a pre-antibiotic age could be fatal. Nonetheless, apart from the obvious human tragedies, these deaths were wholly damaging for the School. Not surprisingly numbers fell. Appropriate measures were taken but it was a question of closing the stable door after the horse had bolted. A high price had been paid for inadequate preparation.

It was crucial that the buildings were completed but the funds simply were not there. By 1868 Woodard had raised £250,000, of which £100,000 had been spent on Lancing and £40,000 on Hurstpierpoint. There should therefore have been ample capital to finance the estimated £40,000 cost of building the whole of Ardingly. In fact by 1870 only £15,459 had been spent and Woodard appears to have been reluctant to have released further funds for Ardingly. It needs to be remembered also that his insistence on very low fees (still £15 per annum) meant that no surpluses could be made to help with capital funding.

The market for further capital funds had dried up. The reform of the Endowed Schools was now beginning to take effect and there was therefore less need for Woodard's boarding schools. Voluntary contributions had ceased. After 1870 Woodard himself was based in Manchester and preoccupied with developing his great scheme in the industrial Midlands and also with completing Lancing Chapel.

In 1873 one last desperate meeting, chaired by Lord Salisbury in Brighton, was held to try and raise funds to complete the work. It had limited success. Now Ardingly was reliant on a few notable benefactors such as Martin Gibbs, who had moved into the farmhouse adjacent to the School, and later in the 1920s Colonel Warren. The School had started out underfunded and was to remain that way for nearly 100 years. Only in the later 1960s and 1970s, and in a very different economic environment, could Ardingly regard itself as even remotely secure financially.

The School in 1879.

The view from the Terrace.

One of the first tasks of the new school was to carve out and prepare suitable playing fields. Over the next 15 years (1870–85) with the aid of a good deal of boy labour, the four main games fields, familiar to all Ardinians, were first levelled and then prepared. One can see clearly today how the Upper (it was to become the main football ground), the Green (the cricket ground), and the Hard (junior cricket and football) were laid out, had stones removed and were properly drained. In addition the River Ouse was diverted and embanked so that the substantial Nine Acre field could be prepared for games. Football and cricket came to play a big part in Ardingly's life and these successful landscapings were important. Additionally, in 1875, a bathing place was constructed in the deep river gully, adjacent to School House, with a clay-lined bottom and bricked sides, and using the natural flow of the river. It was a primitive but much-loved facility.

In 1878, the Terrace was carved out and levelled, leaving a significant drop to what is now the Headmaster's Garden. Later it was paved, and a low wall provided one of the most beautiful school views

Flooding of Nine Acre, 2000, a sight familiar to Ardinians of all generations.

in the world. Financed by Martin Gibbs, it helped to give coherence to the School buildings and to complete South Quad. It was to become a gathering place for people, and a showpiece. The view from the Terrace has seeped into the souls of literally thousands of Ardinians, although often this has only become appreciated many years after leaving school.

Cricket on the Green.

A year later, in 1879, the Green was enhanced further in two ways. Alongside its western boundary were planted 12 chestnut trees. Providing shelter and character they create a distinctive feature to the ground. And in the same year a thatched cricket pavilion was erected, courtesy of Mr Box the famous Sussex wicket-keeper who lived in the village. Despite its relatively short boundaries (and hence not conducive to slow bowlers) it is one of the most characterful and picturesque cricket grounds in Sussex — tree-lined, overlooked by the red brick Gothic school buildings, looking down on to the Hard and beyond on the horizon a glimpse of Ditchling Beacon and the South Downs high above Lewes. The Green has been a source of great pleasure to cricketers and cricket lovers for nearly 140 years.

In 1880 the North School was at last ready for occupation. This was the third of the four wings in Carpenter's original plan and soon it provided almost a separate school for 90 pupils under its first housemaster, Revd F.K. Hilton.

Martin Gibbs was an old boy of Lancing and a great supporter of Woodard and his ideal. A member of the Gibbs family whose business had made a fortune in the Peruvian guano trade in the 1840s and 50s, he used his substantial private means to support building at both Lancing and Ardingly. He had purchased the farmhouse adjacent to the new school

The magnificent chestnut trees on the western boundary of the Green are still enjoyed by pupils today.

The original cricket pavilion.

and, with the aid of the renowned architect William Butterfield, significantly rebuilt it in 1880. It is not clear to what extent he was involved in the School's purchase of River's Wood Farm, with 200 acres, in 1882. Nor is it entirely clear why the School should have purchased this. It had no use for the land but it did desperately need the funds used for its purchase in completing the basic building of the School. Most of it was sold in 1920 for £9,000, of which the School received a mere £500. Here there are some unanswered questions.

And then, in 1883, there was a memorable occasion with the formal opening of the Chapel. Its foundations had been laid when the first pupils

Reverend F.K. Hilton, the first Housemaster of North School, joined the School in Shoreham when it opened and became Headmaster on Mertens' retirement.

arrived in 1870. They remained just that, and a splendid playground for various games played by the younger boys, until sufficient funds were gathered to resume work in 1875. Eight years later most of the work, though not the tower, was complete. For Woodard it was a significant moment in the School's history. Magnificent chapels were at the very heart of all his school communities.

Now the School buildings were to remain largely unaltered or improved for the next 40 years, except for the building in 1893 of the Cloisters in South Quad, thus giving a covered passage between the Headmaster's House and the rest of the School; and the planting in 1899 of a magnificent row of lime trees down the main avenue and drive to the School.

We have seen that numbers fell following the scarlet fever deaths soon after the opening in 1870. The unfinished buildings and very primitive conditions were unlikely to attract parents, and yet by the late 1870s there was a thriving community of 400 boys and 20 masters. Within ten years an astonishing 3,500 pupils had passed through the School, often staying for only one or two years. It was the low fees that attracted custom. They were kept at £15 pa, which genuinely brought them into the range of the small shopkeepers, clerks, mechanics and farmers for whom Woodard had founded the School.

The Chapel, at the heart of the School, opened in 1883. A service to lay the foundation stone was held in 1875.

A piece of the Chapel foundation stone inside a wooden box carved by a pupil and later donated to the School Archive.

Letters written home by Charles Herbert Shaw in the 1880s.

What was life like for the ordinary pupil? The *Ardingly Annals* was produced by the Games Committee and so in these early years was primarily a sporting journal. Diaries and letters provide the best evidence but only in exceptional circumstances have they survived. Recently the letters written home by Charles Herbert Shaw in 1880–81 have come to light. Born in 1866, he lived with his parents and family at Winton Patricroft, near Manchester, and came to Ardingly in January 1880. It must have been a huge wrench to leave by all accounts a loving family home and to travel 200 miles across the country by train, to be left in these austere buildings in the middle of the countryside and knowing no one. He does however seem to have settled in:

2nd February 1880
'Dear Ma
... I know at least 150 boys to speak to and about 40 more by sight. I bath weekly (on Thursday night). I have begun music off Mr Willis. Canon Woodard gave me a shilling the other day when he came to the College
...
We do not have our meals in the hall, we have it to ourselves in our classroom. The potatoes are boiled in the jackets. Mr Hilton is a very nice man. He took us for a walk last Sunday.
I remain
Your affectionate
Herbert
Remember me'

February 7th
I had a bit of skin took off the back of my right ear the other day in a private bolster fight but it is very slight. We have high jinks when the Captains of the Dormitory are out such as letting cannons off in the classroom.

This sort of comment is guaranteed to set anxious mothers worrying. We just hope that 'a bit of skin' is a scratch, and that cannons refer to some kind of fire-cracker or cap from a toy pistol, forever a plaything of boys.

February 22nd
'I had the headache the other night and went to bed at 7pm. The matron asked me to take a pill but I said "No fear catch me taking a pill" because by the time it would operate the headache would be gone. They are getting on with the new Chapel, it is constructed to hold 1,000.'

The Ardingly engine.

March 6th

'*Mr Mertens is very often troubled with the gout. Marbles are all the rage now here. Please at Easter send me a cake and some biscuits in a wooden box like the grocers get their Dry Soup in. If you think I am extravagant I shall cry.*
They allow the Boy's Own *paper here and you might send it me every week.*
We had a football match here last Saturday between us and Brighton Rangers. We got 7 goals to their 3. They play association rules here, not like we play at home.'

And then the news that every parent would have feared.

April 12th

'*The fever has reached our Dormitory. Five boys have got it and it is slowly spreading. All the boys who live in Lancashire have*

gone home except me and another boy from Wigan. Do you think you could arrange for me to come home?
There is a new railway which is being made near us and they are building a station near us. [This was the long awaited Haywards Heath and East Grinstead Railway, part of the London Brighton and South Coast Railway, and the station at Ardingly was 15 minutes walk from the School.] *One of our servitors has been flogged for stealing some chocolates out of a boy's box.*'

April 30th

At least he did have a parental visit.
'*Pa got here all right. I went down to the station to meet him.* [This would have been Haywards Heath since the railway had not yet reached Ardingly.] *Tell Pa that the cake was very rich, so much that I had the stomach ache through eating too much at a time. Canon Woodard came last Thursday. I have had 17 baths as yet. Monday 25th being the Queen's birthday, we had a holiday.*'

The summer vacation been and gone, he returns for the Second Half at the end of July. Schoolboy pranks have not changed in a hundred years or more.

The Boy's Own, *a popular paper for the boys.*

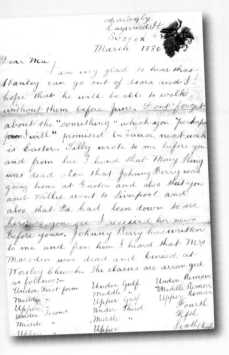

September – no date
'We have rare larks when we go to bed such as sewing the bolster to a boy when he is asleep and, especially when we have got a grudge against him. There are 53 boys in the dormitory now.'

Overcrowding is a constant problem in these years. It will have contributed to the high incidence of disease.

October 16th
'The lower part of the field was flooded and all the fields are like a flowing sea.'

The low-lying Nine Acre with the River Ouse flowing around its edge, and with only the slightest of embankment, has always been susceptible to flooding. Its heavy clay soil has led to very muddy pitches in winter and the long trudge back to the School through the wood with mud-caked boots has been a feature of Ardingly life since time immemorial.

Snow days.

November 12th
'I was gated on that day along with about 20 other fellows for hissing the Captain of the Dormitory because he has made himself unsocial and unpopular.
Cards are coming into fashion and whist and cribbage are the leading games.'

October 28th
'We had a paper chase for boys over 14. I did not go because I am very short-winded and a run of 15 miles would knock me up. The Hares went all over the place, up to the Three Bridges on the LB and SCR about 8 miles off. All the boys came in tired and bleeding and up to the neck in mud, having to cross various ditches, rivers and brooks, and many a farmer had some of his apples stolen.'

There are shades here of *The Railway Children*, not least with the use of the railway track.

How often does it snow today in October and November? Evidence for contemporary global warming come from these entries:

October
'Last week but one (the 20th) we had snow.'

November 29th
'It has been snowing of late and a very hard frost freezing the water about from top to the bottom.'

Some things, though, never change.

'Smoking is strictly prohibited. Our Captain of the Dormitory who is a prefect indulged in it against the rules and was caught last Saturday. He was flogged and degraded. We have a new Captain now.

December 10th

'I shall be home in two weeks and then you must make a batter pudding and some hot stewed beef-kidney.

The Headmaster's wife had twin girls the other week, in all he has 20 or 21 children (this is the truth, no stuffing up).

One Sunday we went out with Mr Hilton and we came to a farm where "swedes" were in abundance so of course we had our wacks out of them, I am afraid some of the boys were troubled with the worm afterwards.

On very cold nights in the Dormitory boys fill ginger bottles with hot water in order to keep warm in bed — woe-betide the boy whose cork comes out.'

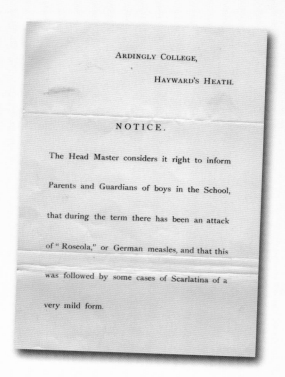

ARDINGLY COLLEGE,

HAYWARD'S HEATH.

NOTICE.

The Head Master considers it right to inform Parents and Guardians of boys in the School, that during the term there has been an attack of "Roseola," or German measles, and that this was followed by some cases of Scarlatina of a very mild form.

He returns home for the five-week Christmas holiday, and then journeys back to Ardingly for his second year. There is nothing eventful until the dreaded fever arrives again.

March 27th 1881

'I have a very sad letter to write to you. Measles for the last six or seven weeks has prevailed and now scarlitina has broken out. Moore in School House died very suddenly last Wednesday 23rd and was interred in the village Parish Church on Friday 25th. On Monday 21st he threw up a little in School and complained that he felt ill. He was taken down to the Infirmary where he died at 4 o'clock on Wednesday afternoon. They say that another boy is very ill and not expected to live.

What I want to know is am I coming home? Fever has not yet struck in my dormitory.'

April 1st

'Fever is still going on — 20–30 boys are ill — five boys are prayed for as dangerously ill. There are only 28 boys in the Dormitory. About 100 boys have gone home. Altogether it is sickening. There is scarcely anything to do — few lessons, no music, not allowed out.'

April 26th

'Some of the boys who have got the fever are getting well, but others are still very ill, only one boy is prayed for in Chapel. It is very fine down here, the violets line the road, and together with hawthorn and cherry blossom and primroses, make the air smell very sweet, especially just after a slight shower.

May 2nd

I am very sorry to tell you that another boy named Rowland has died of the fever and was interred at the village Church on the 28th. All the mattresses on which the fever boys have been lying are burnt as soon as the boy is recovered.'

May 12th

'The fever is going away.'

Presumably he did not go home though we cannot tell why not. Herbert Shaw's letters, written in a beautifully neat and legible hand, speak down to us through the years of a world that has long been lost. Everyday life was closer to nature and obviously less physically comfortable than today. Yet clearly he relished the fellowship and camaraderie of community life in a delightful setting.

The College Cricket XI, 1886.
Billy Newham (centre) and to
his left George Brann and
Frank Blackman.

Until 1885 the year was divided into two halves, from end January to end June, and then from end July to the week before Christmas. Despite the frequent half and whole holidays, these halves must have seemed interminable. In that year the practice of three terms followed by many other schools was adopted at Ardingly. Remarkably at the outset, the Easter holiday of two weeks was optional and not every boy went home. Some, of course, would have had parents living abroad but nonetheless our hearts sink at the thought of boys left at school whilst others went home for the holidays.

Football and cricket have played big parts in Ardingly life, no more so than in the 1880s when the School gained a strong reputation for its prowess at both. Nationally sport was growing fast in this period as living standards rose, hours of work were reduced, and games were codified and organised. The influence of the public schools was considerable. Organised games were seen as a means of channelling the energies of teenage boys into wholesome activities. Godliness and manliness were two virtues of the Arnoldian public school, and Ardingly was well prepared to ape them. It should also be noted

that Ardingly, in common with some schools, but by no means all, played masters and probationers in its teams until the 1890s. Of course most boys left the College at 14 or 16, unlike the upper tier schools where pupils would stay till 18. This meant that Ardingly could only compete seriously with other schools and clubs if these adults played. It could however lead to misunderstandings and accusations of sharp practice.

George Brann, Walter Bettesworth, Billy Newham and Frank Blackman were exceptional cricketers on the Green in the early 1880s. All four played for Sussex whilst still at school. Brann, as a prolific run-scorer for the county for nearly 20 years and England international footballer, was Ardingly's most distinguished sportsman in its first 150 years; and Newham served Sussex cricket for 63 years as player, Captain, Secretary and Assistant Secretary. Their careers are more fully recorded in the Appendix. The School's cricket successes made Ardingly's name widely known.

The enthusiasm of Revd F.K. Hilton and Richard Cunnington, the School Secretary, allied to the expert coaching of Alfred Shaw and John

The School in 1890.

Mycroft, the well-known professionals employed by that great cricket lover, Lord Sheffield, at Sheffield Park, five miles away, did much to help develop Ardingly's game. Because Ardingly's teams contained masters and probationers as well as boys, opponents tended to be club sides. The M.C.C. was beaten in two successive years (1881–82) and in 1883 there was the extraordinary game when the School batted all day for 672, and sent the M.C.C. home without an innings, the declaration not yet having been introduced in the rules of the game of cricket.

The 1880s also saw the game of Association Football getting a hold with the players dressed in old trousers cut off or cricket flannels turned inside out and rolled up, peaked caps, and on their feet ordinary working boots with bars or studs fixed on. Several Ardinians played for Sussex in county matches and in 1885, Brann played twice for England. Still he is the only Ardinian to have gained a full international cap for football or cricket. Leading opponents were clubs such as Burgess Hill, Lancing College and on occasions Hurstpierpoint, although this latter school was less keen on playing against probationers. It was not until 1925 that Hurstpierpoint changed over to playing rugby. George Brann, writing in the *Annals* in 1903, gave a flavour of those early days:

'Possibly from a spectator's point of view the present game, with its intricate passing and scientific combination, is an improvement, but for real downright enjoyment give me an hour and a half's rough and tumble, either on the Hard or the Upper Field, with a team like the Burgess Hill of old, or the ancient heavy Brighton Rangers. How we trained for those Sussex cup-ties, and how hard we tried to win the cup, but luck was not with us. Yet the memory of those strenuous, fierce fights lingers yet.'

Undoubtedly cricket and football were the dominant Ardingly games. The swimming pool was too primitive for serious competition, but athletics and steeplechases, especially with water jumps in the Ouse and Shell Brook became part of the annual calendar.

Throughout these years there were approximately 20 men on the staff, including probationary teachers. Apart from Mertens and Hilton, two need a special mention. Revd Arthur Lewington was a very influential Chaplain and Choir Master from 1881 till 1894. Woodard was insistent that the Chaplain be appointed by, and responsible to, himself as Provost and independent of the Headmaster. This could lead to problems but, throughout his career at the School, Lewington worked effectively and constructively with Mertens in leading the formal Chapel and spiritual life of the community. He was a fine musician and trainer of choirs, and it was to him that Ardingly owes the foundation of its very strong musical tradition. Beginnings matter.

John Bell was another important figure on the staff. He was not a games player but nor is every pupil and most are a long way from home. Boarding school life can be lonely for those who are not necessarily gamesy and gregarious, and Bell created a wide range of extra-curricular activities – chess, other board games, a natural history society, a library club, and debates – helping to construct and develop the infrastructure of a boarding community. People like him were vital as a contrast to the more traditional and games-orientated members of staff.

Mertens retired in 1894. Serving Ardingly nobly and devotedly as its first Headmaster, he had overcome huge obstacles to create from scratch a school community of over 400 pupils. Although not easily approachable, his boys liked and respected him. The School's third tier status and in particular the shortage of capital funding made his achievement remarkable. Very low fees kept the numbers up, though now the School needed to be put on a more sure foundation both in financial and professional terms. A fresh vision and leadership were needed.

The first surviving House photo taken in the early 1890s with Mr W. Sproston, Second Master, in the middle.

The Chapel.

CHAPTER FIVE

Late Victorian and Edwardian Ardingly 1894–1914

The condition of everyday life for ordinary people in London and its suburbs improved markedly in the 1890s and early 1900s. Living standards continued to rise steadily as cheap food flooded in from the New World, aided by steam railways and steam ships. Hours of work fell, not least with the introduction of Bank Holidays and a half day on Saturdays. Improved transport with trams, at the outset horse-drawn, then from 1902 electrically powered, together with the new suburban and underground railways, facilitated commuting. London's offices grew as Britain continued to dominate the world economy. The senior office clerks, superior tradesmen and shopkeepers who worked in the heart of London and lived in its rapidly growing suburbs were exactly the sort of people for whom Woodard had intended Ardingly.

Whilst Greater London was prosperous and growing, Sussex village life remained remote and rural. It was not until the advent of the motor car and coach in the 1920s and 30s that this isolation was overcome. The College with its boarding pupils coming and going by train was an island far removed from local village life.

But increasingly these were also turbulent years as divisions in society grew wider, trades unions began to flex their muscles and the suffragettes campaigned, sometimes violently, for what many regarded as a deserving cause. Ardingly reflected, indeed represented, the newly affluent lower middle classes of London's suburban communities, such as Croydon, Coulsdon, Purley, Mitcham, Caterham, Sanderstead and Streatham. If it had only limited understanding of Sussex village life, it had none of working-class life in the docks and East End. Inevitably it was a male-dominated society, with little or no inherent sympathy for the cause of the suffragettes.

The Reverend F.K. Hilton, who succeeded Mertens as Headmaster, was a Woodard man

The School's beautiful country setting. For many years the School was dependent on the railway to take pupils to and from Ardingly.

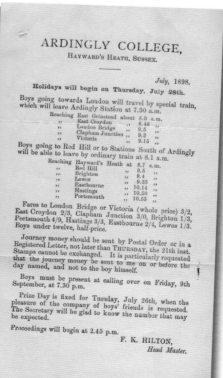

ARDINGLY COLLEGE,
HAYWARD'S HEATH, SUSSEX.

July, 1898.

Holidays will begin on Thursday, July 28th.

Boys going towards London will travel by special train, which will leave Ardingly Station at 7.30 a.m.

Reaching East Grinstead about 8.0 a.m.
,, East Croydon ,, 8.46 ,,
,, London Bridge ,, 9.5 ,,
,, Clapham Junction ,, 9.9 ,,
,, Victoria ,, 9.15 ,,

Boys going to Red Hill or to Stations South of Ardingly will be able to leave by ordinary train at 8.1 a.m.

Reaching Hayward's Heath at 8.7 a.m.
,, Red Hill ,, 9.5 ,,
,, Brighton ,, 9.4 ,,
,, Lewes ,, 9.35 ,,
,, Eastbourne ,, 10.14 ,,
,, Hastings ,, 10.50 ,,
,, Portsmouth ,, 10.55 ,,

Fares to London Bridge or Victoria (whole price) 3/2, East Croydon 2/3, Clapham Junction 3/0, Brighton 1/3, Portsmouth 4/9, Hastings 3/3, Eastbourne 2/4, Lewes 1/3. Boys under twelve, half-price.

Journey money should be sent by Postal Order or in a Registered Letter, not later than THURSDAY, the 21th inst. Stamps cannot be exchanged. It is particularly requested that the journey money be sent to me on or before the day named, and not to the boy himself.

Boys must be present at calling over on Friday, 9th September, at 7.30 p.m.

Prize Day is fixed for Tuesday, July 26th, when the pleasure of the company of boys' friends is requested. The Secretary will be glad to know the number that may be expected.

Proceedings will begin at 2.45 p.m.

F. K. HILTON,
Head Master.

Special train timetable for the end of term, July 1898.

The School's rural location and the lack of comforts came as a shock to many Ardinians.

through and through. He had gone straight into his service at St Saviour's, Shoreham, on coming down from Oxford in 1858. A keen games player, he had been a significant figure in the development of football and cricket in rudimentary form at Shoreham, and then as an important part of school life at Ardingly. A bachelor, he had given his life to the School in the best Woodardian and monastic tradition. He had however been cocooned in Ardingly society throughout, and lacked knowledge of other schools. More pertinently he lacked the aggressiveness and initiative necessary for a headmaster of a large school urgently in need of the kind of dynamic and enterprising leadership that would bring it up to date.

Hilton relied a lot on Richard Cunnington, known as the School Secretary. Cunnington had arrived from Hurstpierpoint when St Saviour's moved to Ardingly in 1870 and was to be a key figure until his retirement in 1917. Administrator, registrar, clerk of works, domestic supervisor, he did everything that nowadays the Bursar and his team do. He was also a fine cricketer, and his coaching and enthusiastic encouragement helped to put Ardingly's cricket on the map. Furthermore he was responsible for planting the distinctive poplar trees which lined the eastern boundary of the Green until the 1990s.

The outbreak of the Anglo-Boer War in 1899 and especially Black Week in December of that year (when the British Army found itself outmanoeuvred by a rabble of farmers and ended up under siege in Mafeking, Ladysmith and Kimberley) shook Britain's

The Reverend F.K. Hilton, Head 1894–1904, served the School for 46 years.

complacency. This did not escape Ardingly and the founding of the cadets in 1902 was an important step forward as the School, like all other public schools, began to prepare its young men for what turned out to be the military horrors of the 20th century.

In July 1904 Hilton retired after a lifetime of service to Ardingly. Of his commitment and loyalty there can be no doubt. Although not a great headmaster, he was a caring and dedicated schoolmaster in the widest sense of that term,

A pupil's report, 1899.

The Masters with Hilton, middle front row, just before his retirement in 1904.

respected and liked by generations of pupils. A few days earlier Mertens had died, as had Lewington the previous December. The three pillars of Ardingly's creation and development were now gone and in many respects the School was at a turning point. The initial Christian idealism was dissipated and although the demand for a good and proper education was ever present, competition from the state was well established. The Education Act of 1902 enabled local authorities to set up secondary schools, many of which developed into the direct grant schools. The parents of boys in London's orbit could now look for local and sometimes free alternatives to a country boarding school which thus far had shown no great academic prowess.

The choice of Ardingly's third Headmaster was going to be vital. The Provost, in whose gift this appointment lay, went for Revd Herbert Rhodes, the son of a headmaster, educated at Shrewsbury School and Christ Church, Oxford, where he had read Greats and also captained the university football team. He was a strong and vigorous character. In the 12 years since graduation he had taught in six different schools, never staying for more than three years in any one. Ordained in 1899, he came to Ardingly direct from a two-year stint as Master of Christ's Hospital Prep School. A High Churchman, it was soon clear that he was not going to let the grass grow under his feet.

Rhodes recognised speedily that Ardingly's reputation for football and cricket, together with its beautiful environment, were insufficient to win over London's parents when there were better and cheaper alternatives close at hand. Attitudes had to be changed. Very low fees did not help and here he found the Society of St Nicolas wedded to the long-standing Woodard philosophy of fees that were within the means of the lower middle classes. By 1911, for example, although Ardingly's fees had risen to £55 per annum, they were still some way below the norm as these figures illustrate:

Aldenham School	*£71*
Berkhamsted School	*£65*
Epsom College	*£78*
King's School, Canterbury	*£85*
St John's School, Leatherhead	*£88*

The Dining Hall where a lunch for 300 was held as part of celebrations to mark the School's 50th Anniversary in 1908.

The Reverend Herbert Rhodes, Headmaster, 1904–11.

The aim was laudable, and although this may have kept pupil numbers up, it prevented any sort of surplus being made which could then be used to develop the essential and modern facilities which Ardingly so clearly needed.

The quality of the education in the classroom had to be improved. Rhodes introduced science into the curriculum, and also Greek and German. Importantly he appreciated the need to improve markedly the calibre of the teaching staff. The School in its first 30 years relied excessively on old boys to do the teaching. Usually they had not been to university but qualified on the job as probationers. Under Hilton, for example, 17 of the 20 masters were former pupils and this, as well, led to a narrowing of outlook and experience. Rhodes began to employ properly rewarded university graduates from outside the community. He was also an excellent teacher himself who was able to interest and excite boys. They held him in awe, nicknaming him 'Searchlights' because

of his prominent glasses and penetrating eyes. Prefects were given more responsibility and no longer did masters play in school teams so that Ardingly could compete equally and fairly with other schools.

The School's 50th Anniversary was celebrated in some style in 1908. The actual day, 12th April, was in the holidays and so celebrations were held at the end of term on 25th July. There was a service of communion at 7.15am, at 9.30am a service of thanksgiving and then later a special service in the Chapel attended by 600 people. This was followed by a lunch for 300 in the dining hall with speeches. Poignantly many of these were urgings of the Cadet Corps to be ready for the future. Prizes were presented and there was cricket on the Green.

Everyday life in Edwardian Ardingly was described by R.J. Manfield (A 1906–11) in an article in *The Ardinian* (the Old Ardinians magazine) of May 1990 entitled 'Eighty Years On':

Fountain, Ardingly College. Nº 19.

School scenes from the early 20th century: Top left: Junior Boys by the School fountain which stood on the eastern side of the Green. Bottom left: A dormitory. Below: The Armoury. Top right: Studying in the Under.

'Ardingly ... was a tough and hard school, isolated in the Sussex countryside, where we were confined for three months at a time with no breaks during term.

The School with its exposed position was bleak in the winter but pleasant enough in the summer. Lighting was entirely by oil lamps and heating by water pipes under the desks against the walls of the classrooms and by open fires in the dormitories ...

In A Dorm there were about 35 beds and at the end there was a barrier behind which were four tables with holes for basins ... The bathroom contained four tall hip baths. The under twelves who came to bed at 8.15pm bathed under the supervision of the House Matron about twice a week. This was a great treat as I think it was the only time we enjoyed anything like home comforts ... Lights were out at 9.30pm and we rose at 6.30am on weekdays ...

Box Day at the end of term was eagerly awaited by the boys. Trunks were taken to the station by horse and cart.

"Box Day" End of Term, Ardingly College, Nº 16.

*At this time all transport was horse drawn so our luggage was conveyed on heavy farm wagons; the trunks and boxes rose five or six deep over the gunnels with two horses struggling with the load. Box Day at the end of term was one of great joy ...
The Dining Hall was by far the noisiest place in the School. I shall never forget the roar of voices as you entered from the Cloisters. Boys sat at long tables by dormitories, a prefect at one end and the humblest boy at the other; the latter filled all the mugs (no handles) from large urns; the tea, called hoggy, tasted awful. The food was plain but sufficient.*

*A great favourite of mine was Mr Jacobs, our Maths master, who got me hooked on chess which has kept me going all my life ...
Among the boys remembered was Gerry Miller (B 1908–14) who was about two years senior to me and for whom I had the highest regard. He was one of the friendliest boys in the School and went on to become Master of Junior School and then Headmaster of Forest School.'*

After seven eventful and productive years, Rhodes left Ardingly at the end of the summer term of 1911. He had taken important steps to raise professional standards, notably in the classroom. This was necessary if Ardingly was to move off the lower rung of schools. There was still much to be done but there was a streak of restlessness in his character and he sought further opportunities. He moved to Cranleigh School where he was to be a successful and respected headmaster for 20 years, before becoming vicar of Iford with Kingston-by-Lewes from 1932 to 1945, when he retired. He died in January 1956.

The Reverend Marchant Pearson succeeded Rhodes in 1911. After two bachelors, it was good to have a married man with his wife, Sybil, as an influence in Headmaster's House. He was a Yorkshireman who had been educated at Kingswood School, Bath. He trained for the Indian Civil Service in London, but then returned north to study science at the University Colleges of Sheffield and Leeds. He taught at the grammar schools of Rotherham and then Bradford, before serving for four years as Second Master at Bridlington Grammar School. He had been ordained in 1901, and then in 1903 was appointed as Headmaster of King Alfred's School, Wantage. His background in science and experience

The Reverend Marchant Pearson, Headmaster, 1911–14.

A Junior School pupil in front of Saucelands.

of these other schools made him a good choice as Ardingly's fourth headmaster.

Pearson was a forceful and determined personality and inclined to be a martinet. Headmasters do however need to make their presence felt, and one of their duties is to stir things up from time to time. Three key and long-standing members of staff – Johnny Bell, William Sproston and H.J. Connett – left at the end of his first term. Pearson was to stay at Ardingly only three years, yet in that short period there was to be much change, including two fundamental constitutional alterations, one of internal school structure, the other of governance.

The dormitories in the three quite separate wings of the School (Headmaster's House, School House and North School) had boys aged nine to 18 years indiscriminately mixed up. Clearly this was not ideal in any social or educational system and in 1912 Pearson turned North School into a proper Junior House for the youngest boys, aged nine to 12, whilst the older boys were moved out into either Headmaster's or School House. G.H.G. Nicholson was appointed Master of the Junior House and was to create its own distinctive identity.

This separation of the Junior House (to be known formally as Junior School from 1949) was an essential measure but it upset many of the old boys of North School. Changes like this are understandably unpopular, but young, pre-pubescent boys do obviously have very different needs from teenage boys and so a separate school unit is essential. Interestingly the state has usually made this break at 11+, whilst the traditional private boarding schools have made it at 13+.

Nathaniel Woodard as Provost till his retirement from that post in 1887 had been in effect a one-man governing body for each of his schools. His domineering personality and, in particular, control of the purse strings, meant that the Fellows of the Society of St Nicolas (subsequently known as the Woodard Corporation) had no appreciable role to play. In any event, chosen for their religious and educational background, they lacked the financial and administrative expertise which its schools so urgently needed.

Faced with challenges from all directions, they needed to adopt a more modern and effective system of governance, involving people with a wider range of skills and experience of life, as well obviously as a love of the individual School and empathy with its underlying ethos. In 1911 therefore, following the general trend in Woodard schools, an Ardingly School Committee was formed. Chaired by the Provost of the Southern Division of the Woodard Corporation, it was responsible for the overall policy and strategy of the School and in particular the appointment of the Headmaster. In 1927 the Committee became known as the School Council and has remained thus ever since. Many schools simply call their board of directors the school governors.

The formal separation and creation of the Junior School, and the foundation of a proper body of governors, were two essential measures in the formation of a modern school for the 20th century. These were significant achievements by Pearson, who

also inculcated spirit and pride in the School. It was a great surprise therefore when he announced at the end of the Michaelmas term of 1914 that he was leaving to become headmaster of another Woodard school, Worksop College. He was energetic and had ruffled feathers but most recognised the necessity of what he was trying to do. It was, too, a difficult time for schools. The war was certainly not over by Christmas. Stalemate had been reached on the Western Front and, although the horrendous slaughter of the trenches was still to come, people had begun to appreciate that this conflict was going to have no easy or speedy resolution. The able-bodied members of staff left to join up and do their duty. Resources were being directed to the war effort. For a rural and underfunded boarding school, the outlook was not encouraging.

Pearson reorganized the School, making North School into a Junior House while Senior boys moved to either the Headmaster's House or School House (shown here).

View from the Terrace.

CHAPTER SIX

Wilson: First World War, Revival and Slump 1914–1932

Thomas Erskine Wilson, Ardingly's fifth Headmaster, arrived in very uncertain times in January 1915, faced many subsequent difficulties, and left in December 1932 with the School at its lowest ebb ever. By no means though was he an inadequate or weak headmaster. Rather, by astute management and resolute leadership, he steered Ardingly through some very difficult times which, incidentally, affected all private schools. And when economic conditions were more favourable in the 1920s he took the opportunity to move the School forwards.

His was the first head-magisterial appointment to be made by the School Council. A scholar of Gonville and Caius College, Cambridge, and 43 years of age, he had been on the staff of Bradfield College for 20 years, the last ten of them as a housemaster. A kindly and devout man, quieter and less domineering than his predecessor, and a good cricketer, he and his wife, Ethel, proved an admirable partnership in Headmaster's House. She was to add much to the School community, not least as a fine violinist, and later as a dedicated Treasurer of the Ardingly Mission. Together, they faced from the outset the problems created by the war.

By the end of the Michaelmas term 1914 half the teaching staff had left to join up. Not surprisingly they tended to be the younger and more vigorous teachers, many of them the university graduates brought in by Rhodes and Pearson. Finding suitable replacements was often impossible and there is no doubt that the quality of teaching declined and with it classroom discipline. Only seven School Certificates were achieved in 1915 which was way below the pre-war average. Some unusual situations followed. On one occasion Wilson travelled to London to persuade a senior recruiting officer to release G.H.G. Nicholson from the parade ground as he was indispensable as Master of Junior House. In 1916, Tindall, the School Steward, who supervised the domestic staff, had to be put in charge of A and B dorms in School House and also found himself coaching football. And all of this whilst pupil numbers were at their maximum. London parents faced with the uncertainties of wartime life, including the threat of Zeppelin air raids, found it easier and safer to have their sons away from home, and often cheaper as well, given the low fees.

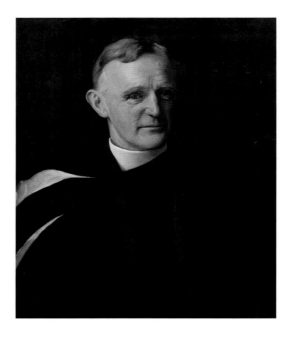

The Reverend Thomas Erskine Wilson, Headmaster, 1915–32.

Soon the community was facing losses at the front. Three Ardinians had been killed by the first Christmas of the war, including G.R. Jenner, Captain of the School in 1914, who died at the front a few weeks after leaving school. The account written many years later by Neville Reed (JH, F 1916–25) was typical:

'My second year started in the Christmas Term 1917 and we had a great excitement then when an airplane landed on the Upper Upper, piloted by a young man, Lieutenant W. Crooke, who had left Ardingly the year before. He had come to say au revoir as he was leaving for the front. Sadly he was killed the next day. We were further reminded how short life could be when news arrived that David Tyrie, who was Captain of the School when I arrived had been killed in Action in May 1918.'

A few of the Ardinians killed in the First World War. Clockwise: G.C Syminton, 2nd Lieutenant, Royal Sussex Regiment, killed in action, 1916.
J. Smith, Essex Regiment, killed in action, 1917.
A.H. Simmonds, killed in action, 1918.
C.F Tweedy, Lieutenant, Lancashire Fusiliers, killed in action, 1917.

Huge numbers joined up, as recorded by the *Annals* in 1915:

> *'We do not know of a single school prefect who has left in recent years who is not serving, save one or two debarred by physical infirmity.'*

There were Ardinians involved on every front of the war. Many who had emigrated to the far corners of the Empire over the previous 20 years returned to Europe to fight for the Old Country. Remarkably, four Old Ardinians living in British Columbia found themselves serving in the same Canadian unit in the trenches, only two of whom were to survive. Even the Provost, Revd H.K. Southwell, served at the front as Deputy Chaplain-General to the British forces.

Poignantly yet pertinently, as Perry pointed out in his history of the School,

> *'It was in these days and years of severe trial that many found strength and consolation in the Christian faith that they had learned at school.'*

In all 1,200 Ardinians served in the Great War and of these 146 together with two members of staff lost their lives. Their names are recorded in the war memorial in the Chapel, unveiled in 1921 in the south wall of the Chancel, now above the West Door.

With so much of the nation's resources being diverted to the war effort it is no surprise that everyday conditions at the School deteriorated. But it was not until the national crisis of 1917 that food

A total of 1,200 Ardinians served in World War I and of these, 146 and two members of staff were killed. The Memorial to those who lost their lives is in the Chapel.

shortages really began to bite. W.W. Mortimer (JH, E 1914–20) wrote many years later:

> *'On one occasion during the war when food was in very short supply he [W.B. Jacobs] caned the whole Junior House in one session because some boy in disgust threw a piece of so-called bread. Bread in those days was pretty awful, one frequently found lumps of potatoes in it; the throwing of this one piece started the whole lot of us and bread was flying all over the place. The only really substantial food we had was a duff. I believe it was 'hardbake'; it was a sort of duff/bread mixture, very heavy with some sort of jam in it; jam in those days being mostly made with swedes with some sort of fruit juice to colour it and give it taste; we got this about once a week.'*

Part of the grounds had been cultivated so as to grow potatoes, beans, parsnips and other vegetables, and this was of some help. There was no doubt however that the diet at Ardingly was insufficient and ill-balanced, although it would have been no better at any other school, or possibly even at home. The debilitating influenza outbreak of 1918, in which one member of staff, Revd A. Keeling, and a maid died, was exacerbated by a lack of proper nourishment.

In all respects 1917 was a very difficult year. Fees of £55 pa which did not rise left the School terribly exposed to the heavy inflation, especially of food prices. Fast-rising prices was an economic phenomenon beyond the experience of most people and certainly of the members of Council of a school such as Ardingly, whose grasp of modern economics was limited.

It was a huge relief when the war came to an end in November 1918. Whit Monday 1919 was a joyous occasion as many Old Ardinians made their first visit to the School for six years. Cricket on the Green between the OAs and the School was a symbol of a return to normality. A few weeks later the final Peace Celebrations took place, as described by Perry:

> *'The religious significance of a great occasion is never forgotten at Ardingly, and the day opened in the Chapel with a solemn requiem for the fallen. The rest of the day could be spent in a variety of ways. Some chose to play cricket or tennis; some caught the early train to Hassocks and picnicked on Ditchling Beacon ("haversacks well filled with enormous packets of sandwiches"); and another party set off for Ashdown Forest, where they climbed trees, caught snakes and picked wild raspberries. All returned at five o'clock for the Swimming Sports, after which there was a supper in Hall. Then came a concert and finally at ten o'clock a great bonfire and more fireworks. From the Upper*

OTC Officers at Ardingly after World War I.

could be seen the blaze of fires in all the heights of Sussex, sign indeed that days of peace had returned.'

It is memorable days like this which see boarding school life at its best. The whole school community comes together to mark and celebrate very special occasions which are remembered warmly by pupils and staff and their families as long as they live.

The School was however very run down by the end of the war and there was much catching up to be done. Fees of necessity had to rise, to £66 per annum in 1920 and to £90 per annum in 1922. Not surprisingly numbers fell, especially when Prime Minister Lloyd George's promise of a 'Land fit for Heroes' did not emerge as the economy fell into depression in 1921–22.

The School's costs were rising fast not only because of inflation but also because of the need to

pay a proper salary to the teachers. As a general rule, half of an independent school's costs are the wages of the teachers. For the first half century of its existence, Ardingly had teaching costs way below the average because so many men served for little or even no remuneration. This was the product of a monastic community and it thereby enabled fees to be similarly very low. Now the School's adoption of the Burnham Scale for teachers in 1921 was an essential move to ensure the recruitment of a proper body of staff.

Soon this began to pay dividends as new and invigorating blood began to appear in the Common Room. George Coghlin (classics, who was to serve from 1926–69), Alan Cree (science, 1925–64), Dusty Miller (maths, 1928–66) and Kipper Herring (science, 1922–60) had the intellectual and personal qualities which were to raise markedly the quality of

Junior School boys sitting on a gun.

Sports Day, 1920s.

education provided. They were to devote their professional lives to the School, help to shape it over the next 40 years and in particular to raise its academic horizons. Other outstanding teachers were Alan Cavill, later to become Headmaster of Hymer's College, Hull and Gerry Miller (B 1908–14) who did much to keep the School in touch with developments in other public schools before leaving in 1935 to become Headmaster of Forest School.

Gradually the economy recovered and for the rest of the 1920s businesses, including schools such as Ardingly, had the opportunity to move forwards. For the first time since he had arrived, Wilson was able to look over the parapet and to the future.

Significantly the School's first purpose-built science building was constructed in 1922 behind School House and, allied to specialised teaching, this important dimension to the curriculum began to be developed. Crucially, too, in 1926 work was resumed on New Wing after a 12-year delay. This project was completed a year later thanks in large measure to a loan by one of the School's two great benefactors, Colonel Warren, which in due course became a gift. Fittingly, the other great benefactor, Martin Gibbs, was present at the opening ceremony.

It had taken more than 50 years for this final part of the School's original five-wing H plan to be built. Headmaster's House, School House, the dining hall, and half of the cross bar were opened in 1870; North School in 1880; the other half of the cross bar, the Chapel in 1883; and now in 1927 was opened the Classroom Block. For the first time Ardingly had spacious, light and airy purpose-built classrooms. This half-century delay reflected the chronic underfunding experienced by the School, and helped, in part, to explain why thus far its academic dimension remained underdeveloped.

In 1926 also the School abandoned the easier Oxford Local exams and instead pupils began to sit the more demanding papers of the Oxford and Cambridge Joint Board Certificate. An inspection by the Board of Education in 1927 gave praise and criticism in equal measure, with recommendations as to how things could be better done. All these factors meant that academic standards were beginning to rise further, evidence of which came with the first awards to Oxbridge, one in 1929 and another in 1930.

There was, too, much going on in the wider life of the School. In Junior House extra-curricular life revolved around the Scouts. Every boy belonged. The camps down by the River Ouse in River's Wood were hugely enjoyed. Junior House boys were known for their self-reliance when they entered the Senior School. In the Senior School, Saturday evening concerts and lectures were a highlight. New technologies added spice to life. The cinematograph created Saturday evening entertainment in the Under so long as the operators were sufficiently skilled; the gramophone was appearing on the scene; and after 1924 all the dormitories had wireless sets. Traditional societies – Debating, Photography, Natural History and Chess – flourished. Boxing was started in 1924 and shooting became a significant activity, so much

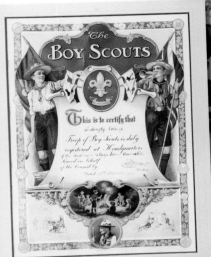

Scouting was an important part of Junior School life.

so that the School team came sixth in the Ashburton Shield held at Bisley in 1928 and received a memorable reception when it returned to school that evening. There were plays and several summer holiday expeditions abroad – to the League of Nations in Geneva in 1928 and to Belgium and Germany in the early 1930s, an opportunity to see at first hand the impact National Socialism was having in the latter.

In 1927 the School was able to purchase part of Merry Farm on the other side of College Road and with it the house which ever after has been known as Frenchman's. Not only did this provide important playing fields, especially for the Junior School, but it also kept developers at bay.

Wilson additionally undertook a series of improvements to the Chapel. The seating was reconstructed so that there were individual chairs for each boy facing the altar; a new organ was installed; Colonel Warren's generosity provided oak stalls and panelling which led to a profound visual improvement; and the introduction of effective heating in 1930 made worship a good deal more comfortable, especially for young boys on cold winter evenings.

Now that the School was moving forwards, it was able to develop through its alumni some of the wider community activities that were characteristic of the public schools. The Ardingly Mission in Poplar, East London, and the Ardingly College Lodge were both launched in 1922, and in 1928 the Ardingly College Scholarship Fund was established. The initiative for all of these came from the Old Ardinians Society with the support and encouragement of Headmaster Wilson and the School Council.

Boxing team, 1926.

E Dormitory, winners of the Efficiency Cup and Year Cup, 1923.

Former pupils had assembled each Easter at the School in its Shoreham days to play football against the current pupils. This custom had been carried on at Ardingly and extended to cricket at Whitsuntide. An annual dinner was held at the Holborn Restaurant in London on the second Friday in November from 1880 onwards. Importantly, in 1906, a formal Old Ardinians Society was established. The war over, its membership and activities expanded in the 1920s.

The Ardingly Mission was established in Poplar in 1922. It had its origins in the settlement movement of the late 19th century in which public schools and university colleges, following the example of Toynbee Hall, helped to set up and support communities in very poor areas of the East End of London. The aim was to provide essential social facilities – clubs, gymnasiums, meeting places – which were so lacking in these deprived areas, and also to build links between young people who inhabited very different worlds.

The Reverend G.B. Ince, an Old Ardinian, was curate at St Gabriel's Church, Poplar, and in charge of the Mission there. In 1922 it was arranged for the School and the Old Ardinians Society jointly to accept responsibility for it, particularly in terms of funding. There were regular visits by the Poplar boys to the School for cricket, football, gymnastics and swimming, and there were also visits by boys from the School to Poplar.

A well-known Old Ardinian, W.H. Cullen, purchased 27 Carmen Street, Poplar, in 1925 on behalf of the OA Society so as to provide the Mission with a new building. This included a gymnasium, a club room with billiard table, a library and a canteen.

For the next 15 years the *Annals* reported regularly on the Mission's activities. Its purpose was to keep 'local boys and young men off the streets' and to 'train them to be good and useful citizens as well as faithful members of the Church'. There was a Senior Club for those aged 16–24 whose activities included gymnastics, cards, darts and billiards, as well as some education. The Junior Section ran a scout troop in conjunction with St Gabriel's in whose parish the Mission stood.

The School and the OAs supported the Mission financially throughout the 1920s and 1930s and Ethel Wilson, the Headmaster's wife, was a notably conscientious Treasurer of the Trust. In due course another OA, Reverend B.M. Lambert, succeeded Ince as the Missioner. It flourished throughout this period until the war brought its work to an end. Being close to the docks, the buildings were initially used as an ARP headquarters until, in 1941, they were totally destroyed in an air raid. Much of the area was heavily bombed, and reconstruction and rehousing after the war meant there was never the opportunity for it to be re-established. Its funds have however been preserved and are now most appropriately used to

Gymnastics display, 1923.

help support the work with young people that is carried out by the Royal Foundation of St Katharine at Limehouse, whose Director is an OA, Canon David Driscoll (A 1957–61).

It was also in 1922 that the Ardingly College Lodge was set up. Modern Freemasonry is particularly appropriate to the Woodard Corporation which set out to build schools to promote Christian education. The Lodges have their origins in the stonemasons who travelled around Europe in the Middle Ages building churches and cathedrals. They preserved standards of workmanship and also promoted the welfare of their members. The Ardingly Lodge, open to former pupils, members of staff and those closely connected with the School, has undertaken much unseen charitable work and also supported the School Scholarship Fund, the Chapel and the Mission. Its annual summer meeting has been held at the School since 1933, excepting 1944 when, with D-Day imminent, travel in the south of England was strictly limited.

Another initiative of the Old Ardinians Society was the Ardingly Scholarship Fund, set up in 1928 to ensure that no Ardinian who won a place at university was prevented from taking it up for financial reasons. In those days there was, of course, no state financial support for undergraduates.

After so much progress in the middle years of the 1920s, it was sad that Wilson's last few years were to be clouded by financial concerns. The Wall Street Crash in October 1929 led to the biggest depression capitalism had yet known. Although the slump hit worst the traditional heavy industries of the coal fields, the impact of falling incomes was felt throughout the country not least amongst the middle-ranking clerks and officers of the banks and financial institutions in London whose sons went to schools like Ardingly. The depression hit Ardingly hard and at the end of 1932 Wilson resigned, with pupil numbers having fallen to 204.

After 17 years he was tired. Ardingly was at a low ebb and needed new vigour, a fresh approach, energy and enterprise. Yet Wilson's substantial achievements should not be forgotten. Almost every member of staff believed in his essential uprightness and goodness. He had steered the School through the great difficulties of the war and the post-war depression, and brought about important improvements. It should never be forgotten that smaller and unendowed schools like Ardingly are very susceptible to the vagaries of the economy; and that the economic and political environment in which a headmaster operates is a crucial determinant of his perceived success.

South Quad from the Terrace.

CHAPTER SEVEN

Crosse: Recovery and Survival 1933–46

The appointment of Ernest Courtenay Crosse was a risk. Desperate situations however require desperate measures. Crosse was an experienced head, a capable priest and teacher, and a man of energy and vision with the strength of character to get things done. He did however have the reputation for being difficult and his nine years as Headmaster of Christ's College, Canterbury in New Zealand had been characterised by controversy culminating in his resignation in contentious circumstances.

Staff during World War II.

Born in 1887, he had been educated at Bedford Grammar School and Clifton College, before taking a First in Greats at Balliol College, Oxford. He then trained for the priesthood and was ordained in 1913 whilst serving as Assistant Chaplain at Marlborough College. A military chaplain in France, his diaries, now held at the Imperial War Museum, provide a graphic and moving account of his work with the Devonshire Regiment on the first day of the Battle of the Somme. He was a brave man and, unusually for a chaplain, was awarded the Military Cross and mentioned three times in dispatches.

After the war he resumed his career at Marlborough and with only six years of teaching experience and none as a housemaster, was appointed to a major headmastership in New Zealand. He was not however a patient man and eventually fell out both with the old boys and, more importantly, his Board. With his wife, whom he had

The Reverend Ernest Courtenay Crosse, Headmaster, 1933–1945.

The School gates were erected in 1938 to mark the coronation of King George VI.

married in New Zealand, and children, he returned to England, obtained a post as Chaplain at Shrewsbury School, and then was appointed to take over as Headmaster of Ardingly in January 1933.

By September 1933 pupil numbers had fallen to 186 in buildings which could comfortably accommodate 370 and had in the past housed more than 400. Morale was low. The Council knew that the significant financial losses being experienced could not be sustained in the long run. Crosse had however faced similar problems at Christ Church with the collapse of the New Zealand economy in the 1920s. At his first Speech Day in December, he announced dramatically that the annual fees were being cut from £100 to £84. He made much of his desire to recreate in the 20th century Woodard's vision of a school affordable to a wide range of people; pragmatically it was a bold move to attract more pupils. The outcome, for whatever reason, was way beyond his, and the School's, wildest dreams. Pupil numbers rose to 287 in 1936, 333 in 1939 and by 1943 — in the uncertain conditions of wartime — were at maximum capacity with 375 boys.

Headmasters invariably claim the credit for such spectacular transformations, and blame external factors when the reverse happens. In fact Crosse was remarkably fortunate. The worst of the depression

was over and the economy had bottomed out in the summer of 1932. Throughout the remainder of the 1930s there was steady economic growth, especially in the South East and in London's suburbs and satellite towns. Arterial roads, the electrification of commuter railways and the development of factory estates in towns like Slough and Guildford helped to stimulate economic activity. City offices, and later rearmament, all created jobs and rising incomes that made the reduced fees of a school such as Ardingly affordable. The motor car, bus and lorry were bringing to an end the remoteness of Sussex village life and thereby enabling the School to broaden its catchment area.

Crosse was also a forceful personality, astute enough to see that rising numbers, albeit at lower fees, provided a window of opportunity for building, an opportunity which was unlikely to last forever.

The north end of Junior House was completed so as to provide extra accommodation, including a substantial flat with a splendid bay window overlooking the Green for the Master and his family. Squash courts were built in 1937, thus broadening the range of sporting activities. A year later a fine and formal pair of gates at the entrance to the College marked the coronation of King George VI. At the same time the incongruous gap created in 1883

The Gym, 1935.

Swimming pool, 1930s.

The Reverend Ince, the School Chaplain, with pupils.

between the Chapel and the dining hall block was filled in with a Sixth Form room above an archway. The recommendations of the Board of Education inspection in 1938 led to a new library (with a significantly wider range of books) in lieu of the makeshift gymnasium in New Wing, and also new science buildings in West Quad on the site of the temporary structure erected in 1922. Lack of funds, though, meant that only the ground floor could be constructed at this stage. The kitchens with some equipment dating from the 1870s were modernised with gas cooking; and the dining hall transformed by the removal of the pillars. Between 1937 and 1940 electricity was installed throughout the School and in particular the improvement this gave to the lighting made a noticeable difference to everyday life.

There was no way Crosse could catch up on all the essential building work that had not been undertaken in the first 65 years of the School. But the developments of the 1930s, although none of them substantial, were significant — indeed it was Crosse's belief that by the outbreak of the Second World War Ardingly was halfway to becoming an efficient modern school.

Although some headmasters are often described as great builders, it is more true to say that good heads assemble around them teams of committed people with appropriate and complementary skills and experiences. In this Colonel Warren, the munificent benefactor, Keir Hett, the architect, the well-known local builder E.H. Munnion (1889–94) and Canon Lea (1874–83), Chairman of the Council since 1926, were the principal figures. Making the very best use of limited resources and a short window of opportunity, they focused and then put into practice the vision of Headmaster Crosse.

School histories are inclined to be written from the top looking downwards, so it can be easy to forget that it is actually the pupils who are the school. Life for Ardinians in the 1930s provided a mixture of experiences, as the recollections of these former pupils attest:

Peter Deacon (D 1936–40): *'Anyone worth his salt and who had not made a name for himself in athletics or some other identifiable field of endeavour sooner or later walked through the Balcombe Tunnel or across the Ouse Valley Viaduct. If you managed to do both you were regarded with due respect, although you ran the risk of being reported. The viaduct was decidedly scary.'*

The School vs The Old Ardinians on the Green, Whitsun, 1937.

Our minds, in this health and safety age, boggle at the very thought!

> 'Our pleasures were few, but one of them was the traditional Saturday night sing-song after prep in the Under. Percy Taylor would walk in, open the grand piano on the stage and we would open our Oxford Song Books and give way together in lusty style. Great favourites were "Roll the Old Chariot Along" and such classics as "The Lincolnshire Poacher" and 'The Vicar of Bray".'

Deacon's comments on some of his teachers are also worth repeating:

> 'We had Beaky Hemingway, Crappy Crawford (the Baron), Boney Barraclough, Clod Coghlin, Kipps Herring, Bin Hett ('The Old North Sea Spy') and the much admired Bill Cree, who was a combination of David Niven and Errol Flynn. Each in their own way tried to pound some knowledge into our heads; it must have been as hard for them as for us. We goaded them, we did outrageous imitations of them but almost everyone had a sneaking regard for them.'

But it could also be a harsh and tough life as the Bonsey brothers, John (C 1938–41) and Brian (C 1939–41) recorded:

> 'The lack of heating in dormitories, classrooms and dayrooms cannot be forgotten – we were chilled to the marrow. The Head's House dykes were open to the sky and there were no doors to the cubicles and no seats (except for one reserved for prefects which had a half door). In winter they were often frozen and unusable for days on end (we had to use the dorm WC). We led such a monastic existence that I don't think we would have known what to do with a girl if she said "Hello"! We were not allowed even to visit shops or make telephone calls.'

Physical privations, rather too frequent and indiscriminate use of the cane, and ample though indifferent food, were accompanied by great camaraderie, uplifting music, energetic and exciting games, and memorable community occasions. It wasn't easy to be lonely and for those who wanted to learn there were some interesting and committed teachers who gave their all to the community.

Old Ardinians had been saddened to see the parlous state of their school in the early 1930s. The Society however remained strong and active. In 1934, with the blessing and support of the School, the old boys' cricket week was launched and then run by P.D. (Sonny) Hawes (A 1918–22), a key figure in the Society for more than 50 years. For the first week of the summer holidays, former pupils stayed in the dormitories and enjoyed a week of cricket against a

Celebrations at the 1938 steeple chase race.

Dusty Miller helping a boy cross the Shell Brook during the race.

variety of visiting sides. Cricketers and their followers loved this most attractive of grounds and enjoyed the hospitality and fellowship of Ardingly, aided by a lively bar and excellent meals in the dining hall. Three guineas for full board and a week's cricket was very good value. Friends and families were welcomed and enjoyed as well the swimming and tennis. It was to prove one of the most popular and successful old boy cricket weeks in the south of England for more than

50 years, until the changing pattern of social and sporting life brought it to an end in 1995.

Another notable though generally unseen development was the creation of the Old Ardinians Trust in 1937. Stanford Letts (G 1918–22), President of the Society, and a member of the Council was the key figure in combining and rationalising under one umbrella several diffuse though interconnected trust funds for the benefit of Ardinians. Another Letts initiative was the Appointments Register designed to help Ardinians in the depression years when getting a foothold in an uncertain economy was by no means easy. The wider Ardingly community was becoming stronger all the time.

On 3rd September 1939, Britain found itself once more at war. This time however there was the benefit of the recent experience of 1914–18. Soon a number of the teachers were joining up but by the adroit use of older, retired and female teachers the quality of academic education did not noticeably decline. Indeed the number of Oxbridge awards rose markedly during the war years. One of the leading teachers, Dusty Miller, was exempted from call-up on the grounds of his role on the land. Composed of a team of 15–20 boys and sundry adult helpers, his 'Land Army' ploughed up three acres of Nine Acre,

Dusty Miller and his 'Land Army' produced the School's vegetables during World War II.

Work on draining the Upper.

some of the land on Frenchman's and the Upper Upper so as to produce all the School's vegetables, and more besides, throughout the war. Potatoes especially but also onions, lettuces, beetroot, parsnips, swedes, turnips and carrots showed exactly what could be accomplished by skilful cultivation.

Dusty's practical skills were of immense value to the School in many different ways throughout his long service. At the outset of war he also led teams of boys in constructing black-outs so that the School would be invisible to German bombers at night. Certainly it was expected that the boys would be involved in the war effort, as Stephen Hobden (C 1930—42) described:

'During the nightly Fire Watch Patrols, Don Rider and I made excursions to neighbouring estates to shoot rabbits. My mother cooked these and then the fire watch teams ate them, together with the official toast and tea left for us in the kitchens. The Headmaster lent some of the "Land Army" to help neighbours with the hay harvest and I was lucky enough to act as loader on top of the wagons.'

In fact there was no obvious tension or fear of war until the spring and summer of 1940. Dunkirk and the Fall of France created the very real threat of invasion. Ardingly in the South East and on the direct route to the Continent was vulnerable. In June, Crosse wrote to all the parents explaining the situation. If the School did have to close, arrangements were in place for the boys sitting the School and Higher Certificate exams to go to Bloxham School, a Woodard school north of Oxford. Others would simply have to go home until other arrangements could be made for the autumn.

Ardingly faced two threats. It could be evacuated if the south of England looked like being invaded or its buildings and estate could be commandeered by a government department be it for military training, for a hospital, or in some other way.

So uncertain was the national outlook that the start of the Michaelmas term 1940 was delayed by two weeks, but with the Battle of Britain won (Ardingly was at its western extremity and witnessed only one dog-fight in the skies above) the threat of invasion receded and the School reassembled at the beginning of October, excited but undisturbed.

A few Ardinians who died in World War II. Clockwise from top left: Lindsay Delacour, Michael Barnes, Derek Whitley, Keith Foster, Reginald A. M. Lemmon, David Wilkinson-Cox, Derek Okey and Richard Jordan.

General (as he then was) Montgomery spent two days at the School in the Christmas holiday of 1941 with a number of his senior officers undertaking various exercises, and although he did suggest he might want to take over the School for military purposes, Crosse was firm and resolute in resisting the idea. The threat of both evacuation and commandeering was in fact greatly reduced after the German invasion of Russia in 1941.

Arnold Hett in his own inimitable style ran the Officer Training Corps (which became the Junior Training Corps in 1940) throughout the war. Two parades a week and regular field days in Ashdown Forest meant that Ardinians were well prepared when they were called up into the armed services.

The War Office now was encouraging boys to stay on at school before joining up at the age of 18. This was one factor in helping pupil numbers to rise to the maximum of 375 by 1943. Another was simply that parents felt it safer to have their sons in the countryside rather than at home in and around London susceptible to bombing. G dormitory, closed in the depression, was reopened and beds fitted into every possible nook and cranny. A school with a long waiting list was a very far cry from that which Crosse had inherited ten years earlier.

Confidence was such that in the *Annals* of 1943, Crosse was able to publish his 'Plans for the Future of

Memorial to those who gave their lives in World Wars I and II.

Ardingly', a document which today we would call a development plan. It was a list of things which could be done without major expenditure — a top storey for the Science Block, an extension to the Sanatorium, a new Common Room for the masters, the panelling of the Under, a gymnasium, and a reconstruction in Junior House. It is right to look to the future, even in the darkest days, and although the funds were not available

The names of those who died are recorded in the Book of Remembrance *which is kept in the Crypt.*

for Crosse to undertake these desirable projects, they all came to fulfilment in the 20 years after the war.

The summer of 1944 saw restrictions on the movement of people in the south of England as preparations for D Day were in hand. Everyone at Ardingly felt the immediacy of a great undertaking, not least as waves of bombers flew over the School in the aftermath of the landings. In reply came the doodlebugs, the V1 rockets, which, although aimed in the general direction of London, were more than capable of going off course.

The very first V1 rocket to fall on England came down only half a mile from the School, as remembered by David Carpenter (G 1940—45):

'We had heard about these new jet aircraft that the Jerrys were using and we were always hoping to see one. At around 2am on June 13, 1944 Mike (Hawthorn) and I (who were next to each other in G dorm) were awakened by this horrible noise which sounded rather like a very harsh 2 stroke engine. "It's a jet!" said Mike and almost as he spoke the noise stopped and we realised that whatever it was, it was right above and about to fall on us. We just about got under our beds — as did the other boys who had woken up — by the time it hit the ground and exploded in Cuckfield.'

Former pupils had, of course, served on many different fronts. Eighty-eight Ardinians had died and their names are recorded in the Book of Remembrance in the Crypt and collectively on the Memorial Board in the Under.

Eventually, in 1945, with the war over and peace restored, Crosse decided it was time to retire and hand on the torch to new and fresh hands. He had served the School well in his 13 years. Older and wiser, he had learned from his earlier and unhappy experiences in New Zealand.

He is remembered as the Headmaster who restored Ardingly's fortunes from their lowest ebb. Cleverly he had taken the opportunity to exploit the favourable conditions of the 1930s. One of his most understated contributions was to continue to raise academic standards. When he arrived in 1933 there were five boys in the Sixth Form. By 1939 there were 25, and by 1946 57. Pre-1937 there had been precisely two exhibitions to Oxford and Cambridge, between 1939 and 1946 there were nine. To his credit new and talented staff had been recruited, such as Bob Hemingway (classics) and Jack Mance (French). Matters academic had now become important, as increasingly Ardinians went on to university. And his election as a member of HMC (The Headmasters' Conference) in 1935 gave recognition to this achievement and enhanced Ardingly's status.

Wisteria in full bloom below the Staff Common Room.

The School which George Snow inherited in 1946 had survived the trauma of the depression and the uncertainties and dislocation of war but the staff was however elderly and depleted. Crosse had run out of steam and discipline amongst the pupils was neither firm nor sound; there had been no building during the war years, and now shortages of materials and money meant that none was in the offing; despite its recent growth, the Sixth Form was small compared to other schools and there were few societies; facilities were lacking — no sanatorium, no gymnasium, no music school. A lot needed doing.

George d'Oyly Snow, Ardingly's seventh Headmaster, was born in 1903, the son of a lieutenant general. Educated at Winchester and Oriel College, Oxford, he had set out on a career as a schoolmaster. Twelve years at Eton, during which time he was ordained in 1933, were followed by ten at Charterhouse where he was Chaplain. He was therefore an experienced schoolmaster when he came to Ardingly — he knew how boarding schools worked, appreciated the underlying psychology of boys, the habits and hinterland of schoolmasters. Quickly he came to realise that Ardingly had possibilities. More prosaically he understood that if those possibilities were not taken the School would either close through lack of custom or be closed by the Ministry of Education for being inefficient.

It was George Bernard Shaw who said that progress is usually achieved by people who are unreasonable since they persist in trying to adapt the world to themselves, whilst reasonable people adapt themselves to the world. Snow fell into the former category. Utterly committed, sure of his own ground, and not given to compromise or any great subtlety, he was an autocratic individual who involved himself in every aspect of the life of the School.

Similarly it was Winston Churchill who once famously said that headmasters had been invested with more power than any prime minister had ever possessed. This too applied graphically to Ardingly's Snow. He pushed forwards relentlessly. Many followed this Old Testament patriarchal figure and there is no doubt that he attracted around him a number of able personalities. He was a visionary with the attention to detail and single-mindedness of purpose necessary to get things done. And he also possessed a deep, abiding and simple Christian faith which drove and informed his life.

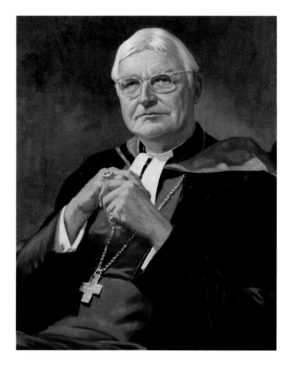

The Reverend George Snow, Headmaster, 1946–1961.

An unusual insight into Snow the man came many years later from his second son Jon, the renowned presenter and television reporter from the world's hotspots, who wrote about his childhood in the Headmaster's House at Ardingly in his vivid autobiography *Shooting History*.

'My father, as Headmaster, was God. He was an enormous man, six feet seven in his socks, and at least sixteen stone. He wore baggy flannel suits in term time, and leather-patched tweed jackets in the evenings. His hands were large and handsome, and skin cracked and tanned. He was old for as long as I can remember

him. *His great height and booming voice
gave him an intimidating, almost
threatening presence.'*

One of his pupils, John Doncaster (E 1945–50), later
himself a headmaster (at The Selwyn School,
Denton, Texas) wrote:

*'As a headmaster he was literally and
figuratively, a giant, an aspect enhanced
rather than minimised by the fact that he
was a somewhat remote and aloof figure,
though that is not to say that he couldn't be
kind, helpful, understanding and tolerant, as
he was to me on more than one occasion.'*

Dominant and domineering figures are unlikely to be
all things to all men and Snow was not one for the
faint-hearted. There were in the early years tensions
with the Council as he wanted to move faster than
they thought wise. A few teachers fell by the wayside.
The Reverend John Gardiner was Chaplain for only
four terms (1957–58) before being 'transferred' by
the Provost to Bloxham School where there was a
pressing need for a man of his experience. Gardiner

Snow was an imposing figure.

felt that Snow was fundamentally a lonely man with
little sense of humour. Ruthless in his quest to
improve the School, he did not find it easy to relate

Old Ardinian reunion dinner, 1951.

The day rooms with desks and carrels, 1950s.

to his fellow priest who had been appointed not by himself but by the Provost, as was the custom and practice in the Woodard schools. Snow regarded himself as both headmaster and parish priest.

There were three principal ways in which Snow set about bringing Ardingly into the second half of the 20th century — in bricks and mortar, in the everyday ordering of School life, and in the Common Room.

First, he was a builder. The distinct shortage of materials as Britain rebuilt itself after the war resulted in a building licence being required for any project. Fees at £100 per annum meant that there were no surplus funds. Yet through ingenuity, determination, no little guile, and sheer force of character, he managed to get much done. His first project was the rededication of the Crypt as a small, intimate, warm and dignified chapel. It was a place of peace and calm, not least in the weekly late Evening Service at which Compline was said, and it was here, in his weekly address, that some of Snow's most enduring spiritual work was done. Crucially, the crude and raucous day rooms were transformed by building carrels into the walls — simple wooden compartments giving individual privacy and a base for every boy — the idea stemming from the study area in medieval monasteries. Today, the appearance would be that of a rather cramped open-plan office. The Science Block was substantially developed with a new floor in 1949 and a new wing in 1957. In 1952 the Armoury was built, an essential adjunct to any successful Combined Cadet Force (as the Junior Training Corps had become in 1949). The new Sanatorium Block was opened in 1955 and the Under panelled a year later. Tennis courts and an observatory saw building across the road in what was now known as Coronation Field.

Between 1949 and 1954 the School built six houses in Standgrove Place, and also purchased several other houses in the village. This had the laudable aim of providing the appropriate housing necessary to recruit able-bodied married members of staff. Little did Snow and his Council realise that they were creating an asset which half a century later, having appreciated hugely in value, was to help tide the School over a period of significant financial difficulties. He initiated, too, the house studies in South Quad which again were to provide modern and appropriate facilities for senior boys.

The Crypt, a spiritual place of peace and calm.

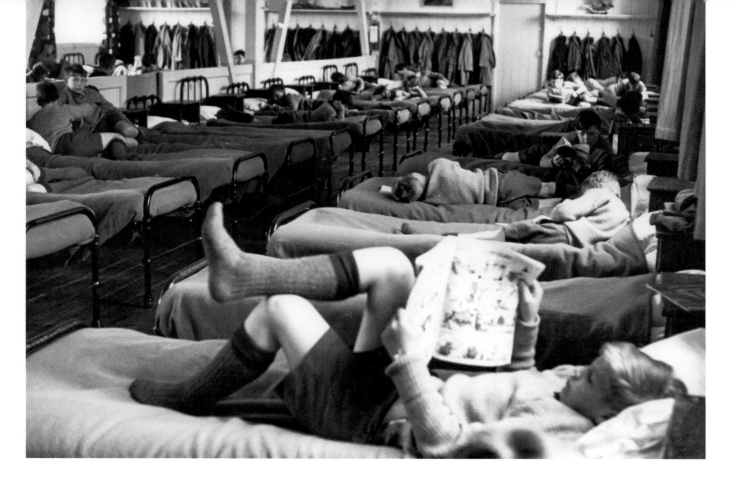

The financing of all this depended on increased numbers, rising fees, the accessing of public funding (for example, the War Department for the Armoury, and the Industrial Fund for the Science Block) and generous benefactors. There was a good deal of Nathaniel Woodard in George Snow. Priests both, they were adroit at persuading those who had the means to support the School's cause. Several Old Ardinians were extremely generous, not least E.H. Munnion, the local builder and father of two Ardinians, who did much of the School's building, often on generous and delayed terms. Ardingly was not always renowned for its speed in paying bills and Snow's speech of thanks at a Christmas Dinner at which Munnion was the chief guest could well have been misinterpreted: 'No one knows how much Ardingly owes to Mr Munnion.' A number of these supporters, led by Stanford Letts, helped to establish in 1954 the Friends of Ardingly, as a society of supporters. For more than 50 years the Friends have raised substantial funds for the School and also created much fun and fellowship, not least among Ardingly parents.

The second way in which Snow sought to modernise the School was in the ordering and construction of its daily life. The long-standing dormitories became proper house units with appointed housemasters and names, although the designated letters were retained for the sake of simplicity:

A   was called Mertens (after the first Headmaster)
B   Hilton (the second Headmaster)
C   Lewington (the 19th-century Chaplain and Choirmaster, one of the founding figures)
D   Gibbs (benefactor; there is also a Gibbs House at Lancing)
E   Rhodes (the third Headmaster)
F   Lea (Chairman of Council 1926–42)
G   Warren (benefactor)
H   Crosse (the sixth Headmaster)

School House and Headmaster's House ceased as units of organisation in the School, and instead the two groupings of dormitories were known simply as School House Wing and South School Wing.

The house system was an integral part of the public school ethos. Every boy had a tutor who saw him weekly, providing both academic and pastoral advice, acting as confidant, broker, spokesman and the School's link with parents. The prefectorial

A group of prefects, 1950s.

Top: *Choir outing to Canterbury, 1953.*
Bottom: *Christian Fellowship Group, 1955.*

system was overhauled, giving the senior boys clear responsibilities. He broadened the scope and range of extra-curricular activities with the development of societies and a spate of activities after 8.30pm.

> *'Snow was a commanding figure, encouraging boys in all sorts of activities. He saw no reason why any boy should have nothing to do – 'keep young people busy and they will not get into mischief',* wrote David Petitpierre (C 1949–58) in *The Ardingly I Remember.*

An annual Expeditions Day in the summer and a programme of Saturday Evening Lectures and concerts broadened horizons. The Pioneers who chose to work on the estate rather than play games in the afternoons were the natural successors to the wartime Land Army. Importantly, Snow recognised the need to make life more interesting and also more fun for young people.

The third way was through the recruitment and then retention of able men on to the staff. Heroic headmasters who revive schools alone in the face of all obstacles are usually figments of the imagination and in any event tend to end up having nervous breakdowns. It needs to be remembered that Snow had enormous stamina – he got up early in the morning and he worked; his headship lasted 15 years and only towards the end did people begin to ask when he would be retiring. He built around him a

team of talented men (and occasionally women), good and enthusiastic teachers, unusual and forceful personalities: people who gave of themselves to the community and wanted the boys to develop and grow. This was observed by John Doncaster:

> *'As the young men who had fought in the War returned to the universities and then to teaching, George latched on to them. People like Derek Knight, Michael Watts, Gordon Wallace-Hadrill, Bob Carrington and Robin Miller were a new breed; young, bright, enthusiastic and stimulating to the young. They had an immense impact on the School.'*

The 1951 staff entry was remarkable not only for its size – nine new teachers – but also for bringing in significant figures such as David Harris, John Craig, Alan Pearson, Pat Molony, Jane Brereton and Ralph del Strother, all of whom were to make Ardingly their

In what became an annual ritual, the masters waited on the domestic staff at a special end of term Christmas meal. Taking a break from serving, shown from left to right: John Craig, Sergeant-Major Godlington, Kipper Herring, Snow, Air Commodore Carter, Mr Crisp and Hugh Cotton-Smith.

Choral Society.

life's work. Allying all these newcomers with some of the older hands from pre-war days — Coghlin, Cree, Mance, Hemingway and Dusty Miller — Snow developed a staff with a forward-looking attitude who were ready for anything. He was wise enough, too, to bring to an end the monastic concept of Ardingly staff life. Now they were properly rewarded financially and, as we have seen, appropriately housed.

Snow realised as well that a small school such as Ardingly could not achieve on all fronts. He wanted it to excel at one or two things and, in particular, music. Robin Miller was one of his most important appointments. Joining the staff in 1948, he stayed for five years before leaving to be Director of Music at Oundle. He built a team of first-class music teachers, transformed the rooms in the basement of New Wing

Dates to remember.

The Minack Theatre
Porthcurno
Cornwall.

Programme
1958.

In the summer, under the directorship of Richard Hamilton, the School took productions to the Minack Theatre in Cornwall.

into a self-contained Music School, worked closely with the Tunbridge Wells Choral Society, of which he was also Director, and this gave the unique opportunity for the School Choir to perform the *St Matthew Passion* at Glyndebourne with Peter Pears as the Evangelist, Kathleen Ferrier (alto) and Leon Goossens on the oboe. Richard Hamilton's plays also helped to make Ardingly distinctive, not least at the open-air Minack Theatre on the cliffs at Porthcurno in north Cornwall in the summer holidays. *King Lear*, *A Midsummer Night's Dream*, and *The Winter's Tale* were all outstanding productions that were first performed at Ardingly and then in Cornwall.

Snow worked his staff immensely hard but they recognised his huge energy and commitment. Some were in awe of him, and a few overawed, but many of his chief lieutenants worked well with him, recognising that beneath the harsh exterior was a soft centre. There was warm fellowship in a Common Room which felt it was engaged in a significant enterprise.

Nineteen fifty-eight was the Centenary of the School's foundation in Shoreham. For Snow it was a wonderful opportunity to show the world that Ardingly had truly arrived. His organisation of the celebrations was masterly.

The Merchant of Venice, Ardingly 1956.

King Lear, Ardingly 1952.

ARDINGLY COLLEGE

SOUVENIR OF

H.M. THE QUEEN'S VISIT
JUNE 9th, 1958

AND

CENTENARY DAY
JUNE 14th, 1958

The highlight of the Centenary was the visit of Queen Elizabeth and Prince Philip, Duke of Edinburgh, who arrived late in the afternoon of Monday 9th June, having earlier visited the recently opened Gatwick Airport and the rapidly growing and futuristic Crawley New Town, both new features in the local Sussex landscape. Escorted by Head Prefect John Joyce, the royal visitors spent an hour meeting staff, seeing pupils in action and finished by admiring the view from the Terrace.

In characteristic Woodardian style, George Snow used the Centenary as an opportunity to launch an Appeal. The aim was to 'complete the Chapel Tower [the roof was still covered by temporary corrugated iron dating back to 1883]; replace the old wooden cricket pavilion built in 1879; put any surplus towards a gymnasium'. Generous donations from old boys and parents, many of them through the vehicle of the Friends of Ardingly, helped to complete the Chapel Tower as planned, and to finance a beautifully designed two-storey Centenary Building, combining cricket pavilion and changing rooms on the ground floor with a social room on the upper floor. This, the Centenary Room, affords some splendid views: south across the Green to the main school buildings,

on all sides the green woods and fields of Sussex, and beyond to the South Downs in the distance.

Centenary Day was marked on the Saturday following (14th June) with a visit from Prime Minister Harold Macmillan who formally opened the Centenary Building. In his short address he said that there were three purposes of education: to know when a man is talking rubbish; to learn the things of real practical value; and to preserve the Ancient Faith and strengthen it in successive generations. If these can be fulfilled *'then indeed in your second hundred years you will have carried out the wishes and purposes of your great founder'.*

For a relatively minor public school to receive a visit from the Queen and Prime Minister in the space of one week was quite remarkable. In addition, a four-page article in the *Illustrated London News* in its 'Public Schools' series confirmed the School's national impact. Woodard had found the site and created the vision; successive headmasters had overcome difficulties and used limited resources to move the School forwards; but it was Snow who had now put the School on the map, given it status, developed a modern and forward-looking institution, no longer confined to the Third Tier.

The highlight of the School's Centenary in 1958 was a visit by Queen Elizabeth II and Prince Philip.

Prime Minister Harold Macmillan also visited the School during the Centenary celebrations.

Appeal brochure showing details of the proposed Centenary Building, 1958.

Unlike Woodard, Snow was well versed in the art of public relations. He was an indefatigable writer of letters to the press, usually on matters to do with educational or religious policy but occasionally straying into everyday practical matters. His early morning 'Lift Up Your Hearts' talks on BBC radio made Ardingly known to a wider public. He lost no opportunity to speak at conferences and to preach. In a talk given to a leadership training course of the Sussex branch of the Red Cross Society he put forward seven rules of leadership:

Never react against criticism
Never have a row
Never make the same mistake twice
Never fight on non-essentials
Never accept defeat
Never leave a letter to be answered
until the next day
Be wise as serpents and innocent as doves

He wrote several short books, *Letters to a Confirmand, A Guide to Prayer, Our Father* and *Into His Presence*, which set out clearly and in a straightforward manner the bones of Christian belief. In 1959 his testament *The Public School in the New Age* was published. The Labour Party in opposition was beginning to flex its muscles and to make threatening noises towards independent education. Snow felt it necessary to try and defend public schools, indeed to educate the wider public as to what they were all about. Read today it appears naive and incredibly dated. Even at the time, many felt that he saw school life through rose-tinted spectacles. Not everyone

who has experienced boarding school life would wholeheartedly agree with the following statement, for example:

'...few boys today seem to view the end of the holidays with the slightest apprehension or regret; homesickness is almost unknown; and you will have to look a long way to find an unhappy boy at a Public school today.'

The boys ran a printing press at the School.

WORK AND PLAY: PHYSICS AND OUT-OF-SCHOOL ACTIVITIES AT ARDINGLY.

IN THE ART SCHOOL, SURROUNDED BY VARIOUS WORKS OF ART: BOYS WORKING OR SEEKING INSPIRATION, UNDER THE SUPERVISION OF THE ART MASTER.

IN THE CARPENTRY SHOP: BOYS ENGAGED IN A POPULAR HOBBY, MAKING SHELVES, TRAYS AND OTHER USEFUL OBJECTS.

LEARNING TO HEW LIVING SHAPES FROM STONE: SOME OF THE BOYS PHOTO- GRAPHED DURING A CLASS IN SCULPTURE.

PREPARING A DISPLAY BEFORE THE ROYAL VISIT: A SCENE OF HARD WORK AND DEEP CONCENTRATION IN THE ART SCHOOL.

IN THE ADVANCED PHYSICS LABORATORY: SIXTH FORM BOYS, AND ONE OF THE MASTERS, WORKING WITH COMPLEX APPARATUS.

A FAVOURITE PASTIME: A MODEL RAILWAY WHICH HAS BEEN BUILT BY THE BOYS AND IS A POPULAR ATTRACTION OUT OF SCHOOL HOURS.

On June 14, following the visit of the Queen and the Duke of Edinburgh on June 9, Ardingly College will be holding its Commemoration Day and will be celebrating its Centenary with a Thanksgiving Service and a Luncheon. The guest of honour at the luncheon will be the Prime Minister, who lives not far from the College and who will afterwards be opening the new science wing—for which there was a generous grant from the Industrial Fund. At the Thanksgiving Service the sermon will be preached by the Bishop of Exeter, President of the Woodard Corporation. The Centenary has also been marked by the completion of the Chapel tower, which was officially opened on Com- memoration Day last year, and by a plan to construct a Centenary Building which would replace the pavilion and provide a place where boys could meet their parents and where Old Ardinians and other visitors could be entertained.

Photographs specially taken for " The Illustrated London News " by Chris Ware, Keystone Press Agency, Ltd.

A SUSSEX PUBLIC SCHOOL: STUDY AND P.T. AT ARDINGLY.

THE KIND OF SCENE FAMILIAR TO GENERATIONS OF SCHOOLBOYS: A VIEW OF THE PLAYING FIELDS, SCHOOL BUILDINGS AND THE CHAPEL.

THE CHAPEL, SHOWING THE ADDITION WHICH HAS BEEN MADE TO THE TOP OF THE TOWER AS PART OF THE CENTENARY BUILDING PLANS.

KEEPING FIT IN THE CHILLY LIGHT OF DAWN: BOYS DOING PHYSICAL TRAINING ON THE TERRACE AT 7.15 A.M.

A GOOD JUMP: A BOY NEATLY CLEARING THE VAULTING-HORSE, TO THE ADMIRATION OF HIS COLLEAGUES, DURING AN OUTDOOR GYMNASTICS SESSION.

AN IMPRESSIVE SCENE OF LEARNING: WORK IN PROGRESS DURING A "STUDY PERIOD." THE INDIVIDUAL COMPARTMENTS ARE KNOWN AS CARRELS.

READING A PLAY BY BERNARD SHAW: BOYS AND AN ENGLISH MASTER STUDY "BACK TO METHUSELAH" AT A LITERARY SOCIETY MEETING.

In 1955 a Centenary Appeal was launched to provide funds for a two-fold building plan for Ardingly College, which was founded a century ago this year. The plan was to complete the Chapel tower and to build a Centenary Building. The addition to the Chapel tower, which can be seen in one of the photographs and which was officially opened last year, was designed by Mr. Keir Hett. Previously the tower ended rather abruptly just above the Chapel roof and no record existed of the founder's intentions for its completion. The structure of the tower is such that it could support only a relatively simple addition at the most, a plain Sussex pinnacle. The Centenary Building, for which plans have been prepared by Mr. Fitzroy Robinson, has not yet been begun but it is hoped the first signs of progress will appear on the site before the grand celebrations of June 14.

Photographs specially taken for "The Illustrated London News" by Chris Ware, Keystone Press Agency, Ltd.

Scouts leaving for summer camp, 1960.

Nor indeed with this one:

> *'Co-education ... is a drastic solution to a*
> *very small problem and introduces far more*
> *difficulties than it solves; with all the*
> *constant contacts now with the outside world,*
> *and the very free mixing of boys and girls in*
> *school holidays, the 'problem' of segregation*
> *is no longer a reality: to think of boys in*
> *Public schools as yearning for female*
> *companionship is an entirely false picture –*
> *it is far too full and interesting a life to have*
> *much time left for such longings.'*

There was an unworldliness about Snow which, although it could be endearing, was also at the same time easily risible.

Pupil numbers had grown from 378 when he arrived in 1946 to 426 in the Centenary Year, despite fees having risen from £100 to £384 per annum. Crosse had wanted to make available a public school education to a wide range of people, in accordance

Junior School boys exercising.

with the Woodard ideal. Snow, by contrast, recognised that in a competitive age parents would only pay for what they considered to be a first-class education; that meant good teachers and facilities, and both of these cost money. A shoestring education might be acceptable for other people's children, that was a decision for them, but for their own, only the best would do. Snow brought the concept of the Third Tier school to an end. Ardingly had moved onwards and upwards.

Fun in the snow by the School gates, 1955.

We need to remember also that Snow, like Crosse in the middle and later 1930s, had a favourable economic environment in which to operate. His early years in the age of austerity were difficult, but the 1950s was a period of substantial and sustained economic growth. New science and consumer-based industries, the City as the financial centre of an expanding post-war world economy, London's suburbs and satellite towns were all growing; and with this rising real incomes meant that each year more parents could afford independent education for their children. The concept of Empire, although under threat, was still strong and with it the fashion for boarding. Thirteen years of Conservative government (1951–64) provided a favourable political environment for independent schools.

In 1961 the Chairman of Council wrote to the Ardingly parents to say that the Queen had graciously approved the appointment of George d'Oyly Snow to be the next Bishop of Whitby in the archdiocese of York. He was 58 and the move came at just the right time both for him and for Ardingly. He was the founder of the modern school. He had put it on the map and equipped it to cope with a changing world. But now was the time for a change. A more sensitive and subtle style and approach was needed to confront the new and very different world of the 1960s.

Joan and George Snow just before they left Ardingly in 1961.

The Music School.

CHAPTER NINE

Bulteel: Consolidation 1962–80

George Snow departed for North Yorkshire at the end of the summer term in 1961 and Dusty Miller, the Second Master, held the fort as Acting Headmaster during the Michaelmas term before Christopher Bulteel, Ardingly's eighth and first lay Headmaster, arrived in January 1962.

After Snow, the School needed to draw breath. It was, too, an era in which certainties were beginning to be challenged. The 1950s had been conservative in all senses and increasingly prosperous. There were however some pointers to the future. 1957 had been an important year for Britain in respect of its relationships beyond these island shores. The Treaty of Rome established the European Economic Community, while the independence of the Gold Coast as Ghana inaugurated the beginning of the end of colonialism in Africa. The 1960s were to mark a sea change in attitudes both abroad and at home.

In the south of England however the population and economy continued to grow, as did the demand of middle-class parents for a good education for their children. Increasingly widespread ownership of cars and efficient operation of the mainline rail services increased the range of commuter towns. Gatwick Airport and Crawley New Town continued to expand, offices relocated from high rent central London locations to towns such as Guildford, Horsham and Leatherhead; East Croydon was redeveloped as a massive out-of-town commercial centre; whilst the Brighton conurbation spread out along the coast and on to the edge of the Downs.

Christopher Bulteel, Headmaster, 1962–80.

Christopher Bulteel was born in 1921, educated at Wellington College and Merton College, Oxford, had served in the Coldstream Guards in North Africa and Italy where he gained the Military Cross at the Salerno landings, and then returned to his old school to teach history. Unusually and interestingly, he had taken a sabbatical to test his vocation as a novice monk with the Society of St Francis at Cerne Abbas in Dorset. In the event he had returned to teaching and in due course he would marry Jenny.

In appointing Bulteel, the Council had gone for the polar opposite of George Snow. Bulteel was diffident, self-effacing, thoughtful and sensitive, with a wry sense of humour, and it soon became apparent that his health was not especially robust. And yet he proved to be just what Ardingly needed, providing down-to-earth and human reassurance and confidence, dignity and the capacity to adapt to a world that was changing fast.

Rowing across the swimming pool during the interhouse CCF competition, 1967.

Painting model cars.

Celebrating a birthday in the Junior School.

CCF Inspection, 1967.

He inherited 429 boys and 18 years later handed on to his successor 586 pupils, of whom 40 were girls and 136 were day pupils. These were significant developments in terms of the future.

During his long tenure Bulteel experienced some of the more tricky challenges of Ardingly's existence. After 13 years of Conservative rule, the advent of Harold Wilson's Labour government in 1964 aroused concerns in independent schools. The Labour Party's manifesto made clear its aim to integrate them into the state system. The Public Schools Commission was established in 1965 to advise on the best means of integration, and in its report of 1968, independent schools were told that half their boarding places would have to be made available to the poor who

needed them. The bark proved to be worse than the bite. Labour was in power for 13 of Bulteel's 18 years, yet in the event private education flourished. Comprehensivisation and in particular the abolition of the direct grant schools meant that competition from the state declined.

Whilst the political threat faded into the background, the economic uncertainties of the later 1960s and 1970s proved to be more worrying to smaller independent schools such as Ardingly. Stop-start economic policies, and in particular high and rising inflation at the end of the 1960s and for much of the 1970s made planning both for fee-paying parents and heads, bursars and governing bodies difficult in the extreme. Nineteen seventy-five, for

example, witnessed overall inflation of 27% and a 38% pay rise for teachers nationally. Astute governors realised that although there could be profitable economics in borrowing to build in a period of inflation, by no means was it guaranteed. The Ardingly Council, rightly, was cautious, remembering that first and foremost its members are responsible trustees of a charity.

It was, too, a period of social change. Long hair and challenges to authority exploded in the Paris university riots of 1968. Boarding communities depended for their survival on a reasonably author-itarian structure. In fact, Christopher Bulteel's enlightened and low-key non-confrontational approach to what challenges there were ensured that Ardingly was not greatly threatened. Under Snow it might have been very different!

Importantly, this social revolution brought with it the beginnings of the gradual decline in the fashion for boarding. The end of Empire and its need for boarding for the children of its servants, allied to changing social patterns of life, led inexorably to the drop in demand for boarding places at traditional

public schools, and in its place the rise in demand for day schools close to home.

It was against this background that Bulteel and the Council began to shape the changes and additions which would enable the School to adapt and move forwards. At the outset, funds were scarce as previous debts were still being paid off. The rather shabby dining hall was transformed by improved lighting and oak panelling generously donated by the Old Ardinians Society to mark the magnificent victory of the shooting team in the Ashburton Shield in Bulteel's first summer term in 1962. The School had come second in 1960 and these successes were testimony to the skilled and committed coaching of Captain Tim Elford and Sergeant-Major Godlington. In 1964 the gymnasium was formally opened by Harold Macmillan. He had stood down as Prime Minister a year earlier and now was able to spend more time at his family home, Birch Grove, just a few miles away at Chelwood Gate in Ashdown Forest. Although the foundations for the gym had been laid by a local builder, the bulk of the construction was undertaken by the Estate Workers (successors to the Pioneers). Self-help was very much

Ardingly won the prestigious Ashburton Shield for marskmanship in 1962. The shooting team was coached by Captain Tim Elford (left) and Sergeant-Major Godlington (right).

Staff Common Room.

the theme, for in the same year a splendid fete organised by Nigel Argent and opened by the actress Susan Hampshire, enabled funds to be raised to finance the construction of a new organ for the Chapel.

A splendid staff Common Room was imaginatively constructed in 1966 above the Cloisters in South Quad, providing first-class working and social facilities for both men and women. And a crucial opportunity arose in the same year when the Wood family, tenants of the Farmhouse, decided to emigrate to Canada thus making its substantial buildings available for School use. Both art and technology could therefore be given spacious buildings of their own for the first time. Much later the Farmhouse was to be developed as a home for the Pre-Prep, the self-contained school for pupils aged three to seven.

In 1968 a new house was built for the Headmaster and his family a few feet from that in the main school building which had been occupied by Ardingly's heads since the School opened on this site in 1870. It enabled that corner of South School to become an administrative base, not least for the Bursar and his team.

The School celebrated the Centenary of its move from Shoreham to Ardingly in 1970. An appeal was launched hoping to raise £100,000 for the development of the farm complex, a new and self-contained music school, and squash courts. In fact it exceeded expectations and topped £130,000. The School's finances were further strengthened as its fees gradually caught up with other similar schools. Whatever one may feel about the end of the Woodard

The 'Great Walk' to celebrate the Centenary of the School's move from Shoreham to Ardingly took place in 1970. The boys walked between the two locations over a period of two days.

Fencing in the new gymnasium, opened in 1964.

philosophy of keeping fees low for the benefit of the lower-middle classes, the fact is that the School now, for the first time in its history, had some kind of financial security. No longer was it a poor relation. It could compete on equal terms with other similar independent boarding schools.

Alan Angus teaching in the new Music School, opened in 1972.

Snow House was built for Sixth Form boarders in 1974.

Subsequently the new Music School was opened in 1972, further strengthening this dimension of the School's life. Another essential change after the first century of occupation of the buildings was the modernisation of the kitchens, not least with the construction of a cafeteria system. Standards had risen. One choice of meal, take it or leave it, and no provision for those with different tastes, was no longer acceptable.

The construction of Snow House in 1974 was controversial. Its purpose – a special boarding facility for Sixth Form pupils – was recognised as desirable, but its location on the former Parade Ground in the lee of New Wing and immediately visible at the main entrance to the School was not. Its box-like structure, although characteristic of the 1970s, was strikingly ill at ease with the Gothic style and ambience of the main school buildings.

The local area, too, was changing. The opening of a permanent home for the South of England Agricultural Show adjacent to Ardingly village in 1967 was to have a big impact on the local economy and also on the local roads at show time! Wakehurst Place as an outpost of the Royal Botanic Gardens, Kew and run by the National Trust became a big and much-loved attraction. And the landscape close to the School was considerably altered by the construction of the reservoir and the creation thereby of a

The School has a strong musical tradition. Pavlos Carvalho, shown here while a pupil at Ardingly, is now a professional cellist.

Peter Hayes and Tim Cole with pupils in the Junior School during a Bacon and Lamb Society meeting, 1979.

Ernest Constable, creative and dedicated Art master for nearly 40 years, with one of the first girls in the 1970s.

The reservoir near the School was built in the late 1970s.

Student Common Room, 1970s.

magnificent lake between 1975 and 1978. Not only was this welcomed by those keen on sailing but it also provided a splendid new backdrop of views, and with the pine forest and steep hills coming down to the water's edge, one could almost imagine oneself in Scotland!

Limited resources meant that Bulteel would not be remembered as a great building headmaster. But in steering the School through and round many and varied political and economic challenges, he

recognised that in time the fundamental structure of this traditional boys' boarding school was going to change. Essentially subtle in his foresight, he laid the foundations for the changes that were to be implemented fully in the 1980s.

Apart from very occasional and individual exceptions, the first day boys were formally accepted into the Junior School in 1967. As we have seen, boarding, and especially in a single-sex environment, was becoming less fashionable. At the same time the steady and inexorable growth of Haywards Heath, Cuckfield, Lindfield and Burgess Hill was creating a demand for day schooling. At first, day places were restricted to the Junior School, but inevitably pressures rose and from 1976 they were also available in the Senior School. When Bulteel left in 1980, day pupils made up 23% of the intake.

The first girls were admitted to the School as day pupils in the Sixth Form in 1972. This break with tradition was a brave move for all parties but it was the way forwards for many similar schools at this time. Again attitudes in society were changing fast. A male dominated world was no longer the norm, smaller families and rising expectations for women in all aspects of life led to much greater sex equality. Co-education at school and at university and equal

Top left: Boys with Boris, the School snake, 1971.
Bottom left: Rehearsing Gogol's The Government Inspector with Colin Temblett-Wood.
Top right: Tricky choices in the Tuck Shop, 1978.
Bottom right: David Harris teaching students the finer points of physics, Ian Hislop is on the left.

opportunities in the work place were becoming a reality. No longer were schools like Ardingly islands, increasingly they reflected society.

A headmaster is responsible not only for the physical environment but also for the atmosphere of the community. For any child and most parents that is actually the key issue. Christopher Bulteel aided by some capable and sympathetic teachers ensured that the 60s and 70s were, for the most part, happy and good times for a pupil to be at Ardingly. Personal reminiscences do not tell the whole picture but they do help to provide a flavour. One would not necessarily expect artistic and non-games playing people such as composer Stephen Oliver (G 1963–67) and satirist and *Private Eye* editor Ian Hislop (JH, A 1968–77) to enjoy conventional boarding school life.

Oliver: *'The prefects and the people who really gave the tone of civility to the School were themselves civil men. I was not good at games and it didn't matter at all, whereas it mattered very much at my prep school. I don't remember any bullying in my time; I am not looking through rose-tinted spectacles, it was thought of as absolutely infra-dig to bully.'*

Hislop: *'It was an excellent place for letting you get on with whatever you fancied doing. I made a lot of friends there that I've kept for life.... I wasn't a great sportsman, but found time for lots of other things — acting, writing sketches and performing reviews; I found it all very stimulating — I always remember the sense of humour at Ardingly as quite cutting and there also seemed to be a lot of lunacy, as when Nick Newman and Simon Parke*

Taking off through the School gates for a bicycle trip in the surrounding countryside during the 1970s.

Junior boys skiing at the School, 1977.

organised a roller bike event round the Front Quad and ran a commentary from the Chapel Tower.'

The Headmaster himself in his regular letter in the *Annals* and on major public occasions set out clearly and sympathetically what was the scope of a Christian education in contemporary society. This, for example, is what he said on Speech Day in 1972:

'Ardingly is a small school — worship, the appreciation of the work of others and the gifts they make to the common treasury — integrity, a man's word is his bond.... There are opportunities here for the development of latent talents, and our hope is that our pupils will make use of the facilities that are available; for if they are to achieve happiness in this world, they will do so by living life abundantly, making use of

all the faculties they have developed and sharpened at school and at home, in their youth, and by using these without stint for the service of mankind in the years that lie ahead.'

In a fast-moving and challenging world, 18 years is a long time to remain in post as a chief executive, and towards the end, Bulteel was tired. He had however steered the ship through some choppy waters. His obvious humanity and concern for people as individuals meant that he was highly regarded and that there was a happy and civilized atmosphere in the School. He passed on to his successor a strong team in the Common Room and the opportunity to move and shape the School in a new political regime which supported independent education, not least with the Assisted Places Scheme.

A service in the Chapel taken by the Reverend Alan Cole with the Reverend Nick Waters assisting.

The Cricket pavilion with the Centenary Room above.

CHAPTER TEN

Flecker: Restructuring 1980–98

Thatcher's Britain was good for independent schools, especially in the south of England. The economy was being transformed, taxes reduced, private enterprise encouraged, in a global economy education was seen as more important than ever, and the state provided no evidence that it could match the increasingly professional independent schools. Ardingly likewise was to prosper but in unexpected ways.

James Flecker, the School's ninth Headmaster, brought about not only an increase in pupil numbers but also the most profound structural change in the history of the School, as the figures below illustrate.

The introduction of full co-education, the increasing proportion of day pupils as boarding declined and the founding of the Pre-Prep were fundamental shifts in the composition of the pupil body. Ardingly had been exclusively a male boarding community from its foundation in 1858 till the early 1970s. Remote and almost monastic in style, with worship in Chapel at the heart of its life, the School had put particular emphasis on traditional games such as football and cricket. Twenty years later by the 1990s it was a markedly different institution — co-educational throughout, day as well as boarding pupils, and providing education throughout the school years from age 3 to 18. Although games were still important, there was now a far more balanced programme of extra-curricular activities. A majority of day pupils, and especially the Pre-Prep in the Farmhouse, meant that parents, especially mothers, and their cars, had become a significant twice-daily part of Ardingly life.

It should be noted that Ardingly was not unique in undertaking these structural alterations. Similar measures were being taken by many other independent schools as they, too, adapted to a changing market place in which boarding was less popular and schools which could take all the children

James Flecker, Headmaster 1980–98.

in the family were advantageous to the hugely increased number of working mothers.

James Flecker was a talented, energetic and creative headmaster. An Oxford classicist, England hockey international and enthusiastic musician and producer of plays, he taught first at Latymer Upper School, then for 12 years at Marlborough, where he was a housemaster for six years. A public school housemaster with 50–60 teenagers living under one roof is in effect a mini-headmaster, dealing directly with parents, discipline, a budget, other colleagues

	Total Pupils	Boys	Girls	Boarding	Day	Pre-Prep	Junior School	Senior School
1980	586	546	40	450	136	–	172	414
1998	664	375	289	330	334	83	150	431

110

Fete on the Green, 1998

and often also responsible for recruitment to the house. His wife, Mary, was also a very great asset, not only for the significant part she played in supporting the female pupils but also making things happen in the community that emanates from the Headmaster's House.

It is worth pausing at this stage to consider the role of the wives of Ardingly's headmasters. Living with their families in the physical heart of the campus, there is little privacy, interestingly described from a child's point of view by Jon Snow in the first chapter of his autobiography. Husbands and fathers are permanently on call during term time and for much of the holidays as well. In the post-war period, Joan Snow, Jenny Bulteel and Mary Flecker all helped to build a warm, friendly and welcoming community, making it their job especially to get to know the families of members of staff and to be supportive without being intrusive. Joan Snow never forgot a child's birthday. Jenny Bulteel was a kind and ever-present friend to all. Mary Flecker's weekly morning coffee gatherings and creches were greatly appreciated by the staff wives. All three gave of themselves freely and without stint and in many different ways created a very special atmosphere.

Lack of endowment has meant that Ardingly has never been a wealthy school. Although numbers were not a problem when Flecker arrived, complacency was not an option. To survive and grow in a rapidly changing market place, Ardingly needed to anticipate, adapt and innovate. Flecker was imaginative, developed an excellent and productive relationship with the wise, far-seeing and hugely committed Chairman of Council, Michael Toynbee, and put in motion three key projects

Mary Flecker's weekly coffee mornings were greatly appreciated by staff wives.

— the introduction of full co-education, the transfer of the Upper Sixth into Woodard, and the launching of the Pre-Prep in the Farmhouse buildings. These changes were substantial and were also absolutely vital for the future strength of Ardingly.

Marlborough had been one of the first traditional boys' schools to introduce girls in 1968. Ardingly had been considered adventurous to introduce day girls in the Sixth Form in 1972, but there were only 40 of them when James Flecker arrived in 1980. The School had made no real attempt to build female numbers. The Council did not have a strong view on co-education one way or the other but a headmaster has the power to persuade. Flecker argued that a full quota of girls (i.e. approximately 50% of the pupil body) was essential

not so much for economic reasons but rather on academic grounds. He realised that in the highly competitive Sussex/Surrey market place Ardingly needed to raise its academic reputation.

In September 1982, therefore, girls were admitted to Shell (Year 9 in National Curriculum parlance). There were only nine of them and organising sports teams was not easy. They were all day girls. A year later, however, the first girls' boarding house, Woodlands, opened with 15 girls. By 1984 there were girls in every year in the Senior School. Soon word was going round that an Ardingly education was equally available to daughters as well as to sons.

The planning and structuring of a move to full co-education in any school community is rarely easy or straightforward. For the most part boys and especially old boys don't like it. They tend to be conservative. Their patch is being infringed. Assuredly they believe football and cricket will suffer. Flecker was able to provide clear thinking and sensitivity in assuaging their fears.

In 1985 an extension to Woodlands was built so that now there were two girls houses, Woodlands South School and Woodlands School House. A year later girls were admitted into the Junior School and speedily they came to constitute about 40% of Junior School pupils. Naturally they then fed through into the Senior School. By the end of the 1980s Ardingly was established as a fully fledged co-educational school.

The second plank in the restructuring was the creation of Woodard. Increasing numbers of girls and also day pupils of both sexes led inevitably to a reordering of the long-established house structure, so that eventually there were four houses for boys: Mertens, Hilton, Rhodes and Crosse, and four for girls: Toynbee, Aberdeen, Bulteel and Neal. All these houses had both day and boarding pupils. From 1988, however, they did not include boarders in their last (Upper Sixth) year. Instead, they now spent their final year in the School in a separate co-educational house, Woodard, built specifically for them in the field overlooking the Farmhouse. Designed as a stepping stone between school and university, it was an imaginative project created by Flecker and its first

By the end of the 1980s Ardingly was fully coeducational; School discotheque, Junior School prize giving, Guides experiencing life on the streets.

Footballers on their way to the Upper as autumn leaves fall.

housemaster, Colin Temblett-Wood. Views on taking these senior pupils out of the mainstream house system were mixed. Few doubted, however, that the tensions that can develop when young adults are confined in a conventional boarding community were reduced.

The opening of the Pre-Prep in the Farmhouse in 1993 was the third plank in this restructuring. A separate school for three- to seven-year-olds enabled local day parents to have all their children at school on the one campus. In a modern life of complex car journeys for mothers this was essential. The Farmhouse location was ideal — set apart from the main school buildings, secure, self-contained in a delightful country environment, and easy to park. Sue Vermeer, its founding head, was just the right person — warm and friendly but with the firm grip necessary to win the confidence of the mothers of young children. Her role in getting this important venture off the ground was considerable.

There was no doubting Flecker's energy and enterprise. He was at his desk not long after dawn and from it emanated ideas — many of them! He also appreciated the need for down-to-earth practicality and here his appointment of Martin Cannings as

The Farmhouse.

Deputy Head was masterly. The number two in a vibrant school such as Ardingly plays an important role in ensuring the efficient and effective day-to-day running of the ship. Derek Knight had been a tower of strength as a capable and fair-minded chief lieutenant to Christopher Bulteel from the death in office of Dusty Miller in 1966 to his own retirement a

Martin Cannings and James Flecker with Prefects, 1984.

year into Flecker's headship. Now Cannings was to serve for 19 years. Showing a sharp eye for detail, he set high expectations, was always positive and level-headed, and ensured sound discipline and effective systems, so that the School ran smoothly. This enabled the Head to concentrate on the wider strategic issues and on matters of high politics and finance.

George Snow, as mentioned earlier, set out to develop one or two areas in which the School could excel. Music, his own love, was an obvious choice and an outstanding Director, Robin Miller, helped to put Ardingly on the map. His successors Paddy Forbes and Alan Angus had built very successfully on this foundation, affirming its national standing. Likewise Richard Hamilton and then Colin Temblett-Wood developed the School's drama to a high level. From the 1960s to the 1980s the latter's huge commitment to detail in every aspect of production, created a series of memorable performances. He started with *St Joan*, then *The Crucible* and *The Royal Hunt of the Sun*. Alison Sutton and Chris Gunness (later a renowned television reporter and presenter) were outstanding in the lead roles in *Romeo and Juliet*. Christopher Bostock and John Tolputt gave fine comic performances of technical assurance and vitality in *The Rivals* and *The Alchemist*. The boarding community rose to the occasion of such productions and relished the vitality, imagination and range of the Ardingly stage.

James Flecker, appreciating this need to excel, concentrated not only on sustaining the reputation in music and drama, but also on developing further the sporting prowess of the School. He did this in several different ways. Facilities were certainly improved with the construction of an all-weather hockey pitch on Frenchman's; the building of new tennis and squash courts, following the appeal in 1984; a new, heated and enclosed swimming pool on the site of the open-air pool which had served the School since 1875; better drainage of Nine Acre so that water flowed into, rather than from, the River Ouse; and in due course a splendid Sports Hall in Fellows' Garden.

Sporting scholarships enabled the recruitment of some outstanding games players and, for a decade or so, Ardingly's football was stronger than it had been since the heyday of the 1880s. The architect of this was Graham Dawtrey, long-standing housemaster of Warren and immensely enthusiastic and committed master in charge of football. A four-week tour of South America in 1991, the winning of the Independent Schools Cup in 1998, and, quite remarkably, the winning of the English Schools Football Association Cup a year later, put the School on the nation's sporting map. Several of these boys went on to play professionally, the best known being Adam Virgo who made his name with Brighton and Hove Albion, and was then transferred to Glasgow Celtic for £1m in 2005.

Flecker placed great emphasis on sport and did much to improve the School's sporting facilities. Clockwise from top left: Sailing on the Reservoir, Athletics and Mountain Boarding on the South Downs.

A new, indoor swimming pool was built, replacing the outdoor pool that had served the School since 1875.

Flecker recognised, too, the need for young Ardinians to experience and understand the increasing importance of Europe in the nation's life. The English for Young Europeans (EYE) scheme attracted a number of able German students to the Sixth Form, albeit for short spells. Exchanges with Baden Baden, Toulouse and Pamplona exposed Ardinians to European life at first hand.

Flecker, like Crosse in the 1930s, and Snow in the 1950s, took the window of opportunity in the 1980s to build for the future. Very small annual surpluses, a successful appeal and a favourable outlook for borrowing, enabled an expansionist programme of building in accordance with the long-term plan drawn up in 1983. This was to cost £1.5m and the 1984 appeal orchestrated by Nigel Argent raised more than half of this. As well as the sporting facilities, a new floor was built on top of the Science Block; Woodard was the biggest single building since the Chapel had been completed a hundred years earlier; improvements were made to the Junior School dormitories; a new floor was added to the Sanatorium which then became Wilson, a Sixth Form boarding block; and a new smaller San was created in 1 and 2 Fellows' Garden. This was wise investment for the future, improving facilities which were essential in persuading parents to commit their children's education to Ardingly when there was a wide range of choices.

What goes up must come down, and the recession of the early 1990s hit independent schools

During Flecker's time, soldiers from The Ghurka Regiment came twice to Ardingly to Beat Retreat. School staff and pupils remember the ranks of Ghurkas marching through the School arch at sunset as an impressive spectacle.

hard and especially those like Ardingly which were in the countryside and had a significant boarding dimension. Retrenchment in industry, a stock market fall and rising interest rates meant not only job losses and falling real incomes, but also less confidence in the future. All of these affected the Ardingly parents and some of them faced with the alternative of lower fees at some of the day schools or no fees at all with the state, voted with their feet. Numbers in the Senior School fell. With loans on some of the building projects still to be paid off, Ardingly experienced difficult economic problems. It had, of course, been there before with the lack of capital funds after the move from Shoreham in 1870, during the two world wars, and in particular in the depression of 1930–32, when numbers had fallen to their lowest ever. It was also some consolation that many other independent boarding schools were suffering in the same way.

Nonetheless, drastic measures had to be taken. Fewer pupils need fewer teachers and a programme of staff reduction achieved in part by natural wastage (not replacing teachers who retired or left for promotion) steered the School through the immediate crisis. Such rationalisation of any business also speeds up the process of natural change, and the opening of the Pre-Prep gave the School a new and

important dimension to its position in the market place. And very importantly for the School in the long term, Ardingly Projects Ltd was set up in 1993 under the directorship of Graham Dawtrey. The School recognised that its buildings and facilities were empty during the school holidays and especially for seven weeks in the summer. Reasonable accommodation, abundant playing fields and facilities, classrooms and a location only 30 miles from London and 15 from the coast at Brighton meant that Ardingly was ideal for summer camps, especially for those coming from abroad. Soon the School in the summer vacation was full of young people from all over the world. This may not have been appreciated by those members of the staff who lived on the campus and essential maintenance could not be undertaken in this off-peak school season, but the substantial income brought in each year was absolutely essential to the long-term future of the School. Ardingly Projects Ltd has been a highly successful commercial subsidiary enabling the School to cope with the recession of the 1990s, and then to undertake essential improvements to the fabric and facilities.

In 1986 Roger Grove Smith (JH, C 1937–45) retired after 19 productive and successful years as

David Fairhurst working with the Scouts.

Adventure Training on Mull.

Master of the Junior School. Arriving in 1967 after seven years as a headmaster in Teheran, his civilised regime provided a stimulating and supportive start in life for many young Ardinians. His plays were legendary, not least three tremendous productions of Oliver, and it is no coincidence that three outstanding schoolboy actors, Adam Blackwood (JH, G 1968–77), Christopher Gunness (JH, G 1969–76) and Ian Hislop (JH, A 1968–77), first made their mark on his stage. The annual ski trips, like the long-standing Scouts, became another feature of Junior School life. There were physical changes, too, as meals were taken in the main school dining hall when it moved over to

Flecker with Mertens Sixth form and house staff.

a cafeteria system in 1971, thus freeing up the long-serving Junior School dining room as an assembly hall. In addition, several spacious classrooms in the Old Tuck Shop and Hangar were developed.

Created in 1912 as the Junior House, the Junior School (as it had become known in 1949) had always been in a slightly anomalous position. Amongst some people there was a tendency to see it simply as the junior department of the much greater whole school. It was, after all, just one wing of the five-block main building. When *The Martlet*, its own termly magazine, first appeared in 1958, for example, the Council was concerned that the Junior School's separate identity would be over-emphasised. Grove Smith, however, working closely with both Bulteel and Flecker, was adroit at creating a distinctive entity geared to the needs of young boys and girls of seven to 13 years, yet at the same time appreciating its part in the whole with access to a wide range of outstanding Senior School facilities. The Junior School's own dedicated and specialist team of teachers, notably Maurice Barraclough (1935–40, and 1945–80), Hugh Cotton-Smith (1947–80), John Spear (1950–85), Tim Elford (1954–86), John Cope (1961–97) and Peter Hayes (1971–96) helped, too, in creating a fine and popular school in its own right.

James Flecker, like his predecessor, served for 18 years, his enthusiasm and creativity never waning.

In his first decade conditions were favourable, crucial structural changes undertaken and much building work accomplished. A modern and well-equipped school was the result and enabled Ardingly not only to ride, barring the odd financial alarm, the recession of the early 1990s, but also to take advantage of the subsequent upward trend in the economy. Like all his predecessors, he had committed himself hugely to the School and its life and moved it forwards significantly.

Junior pupil in Twelfth Night.

James Flecker at his leaving party in 1998.

A word from the coach on the Upper.

CHAPTER ELEVEN

Franklin: Into the 21st Century 1998–2007

For its tenth Headmaster, the Council looked to Australia. John Franklin, aged 45, was a Queenslander who knew England well, having taught at both Sedbergh and Marlborough. At the time of his appointment he was Deputy Head of St Peter's, Adelaide; and with him came his wife, Kim, a qualified teacher, and an ebullient and warm personality. They made a good team. Subsequently described by the *Good Schools Guide* as 'friendly, communicative and with a sparkling wit lurking behind a slightly un-Australian reserve', Franklin brought the open-mindedness, combined with clear thinking and steely resolution, which was to serve Ardingly well.

His inheritance was not straightforward. The recession of the early 1990s had brought economic problems. A number of pupils were on the state Assisted Places Scheme which, although very much in the spirit of Woodard, was about to be phased out by the recently elected Labour government. Increased bureaucratic regulation was putting pressure on day-to-day systems. Schools now needed to demonstrate with the appropriate written policies and procedures that they were well-ordered and run on consistent principles. Parents had become more demanding. Ardingly was not the only rural boarding school to face numbers problems and the consequent financial deficits, but, fortunately for the School, the new Headmaster and his team were prepared to face the challenges that lay ahead.

Franklin's first report to Council in October 1998 set out clearly the situation as he saw it:

John Franklin, Headmaster 1998–2007.

'The School does have many strengths including its magnificent setting, its capable and dedicated staff and its friendly, unpretentious students. The members of the School community are in good heart and there is tangible support for whatever positive change is required to ensure that the School flourishes in the next Millennium. There are, inevitably, problems to be addressed as well; while the academic and sporting programmes at Ardingly are working very well indeed, three aspects of the School concern me:
– The structure of the boys' boarding houses
– The poor state of repair of many of our buildings and
– The decline in Senior School numbers

Ardingly exists in a highly competitive market place and if we are to compete successfully against our rivals, then prospective parents visiting the School for the first time must perceive that we offer a quality educational 'product', where excellence is actively pursued in every facet of our operation.'

A modern-day headmaster of a rural boarding school is judged in particular by his recruitment of pupils. Franklin inherited 431 in the Senior School and passed on 474 to his successor nine years later. A concerted marketing operation, wooing of

The start of a Charity Balloon Race, 2006.

prep-school heads, and successful international recruitment ensured that the demise of the Assisted Places Scheme was overcome. At the end of the day, however, the two key factors in enabling a fee-paying school to fill its places are the quality of the education provided and the ability of the parents to pay. Franklin's astute leadership helped greatly to improve the former, and the adroit management of the British economy by Messrs Blair and Brown ensured that his nine-year headship was accompanied by uninterrupted economic growth. Franklin used this opportunity well.

All heads want to build. Any successful business needs to invest in new and better facilities. They do however need financing. An important change in the structure of governance took place in 1998 when the Southern Division of the Woodard Corporation was disbanded. The individual schools were incorporated, which gave them much greater autonomy and also a significant windfall as the funds of the Division were distributed amongst its members. Developing this

opportunity by skilful financial management, together with the confidence and capacity to borrow and a close partnership between Headmaster, Bursar and a committed and far-seeing Council, enabled Ardingly to improve and enhance its basic facilities. Most important were the two splendid new boarding houses built on the edge of Kiln Wood. Four-bed rooms for boys in Shell, doubles in the Remove, and single study bedrooms thereafter, plus well-resourced common rooms, ICT and bathroom facilities, which met the rigid standards of the Social Services inspectors, were not cheap at a cost of £4m. They were essential however if Ardingly was to continue to attract boarders, especially from Europe, in a highly competitive market. It was a far cry from the traditional large and very basic dormitory that had housed the boys from the School's foundation.

A second major project designed specifically to establish a niche in one particular segment of the market place was the construction of a new Pre-Prep building on the Farmhouse site. The importance of

the Pre-Prep in Ardingly's structure should not be underestimated. Founded in 1994 with 25 boys and girls in its first year, now it had 85 and constituted some 12% of Ardingly's pupils. Satisfy the parents, and in particular the mothers, at this stage and their children will move on to the Junior School and then the Senior School. The Ardingly brand is an important concept. Again, however, this is a highly competitive market — facilities need to be smart, modern, and efficient — so the School's plan aimed to create a wow factor in this most impressive of locations.

The programme of building modernisation under John Franklin was unceasing. The School's facilities and equipment were expanded and enhanced — a splendid new music recital room eagerly awaited for 25 years and now made possible by the generosity of Tim Elford who had joined the staff in 1950 and was still going strong; a revamped library; two drama studios; more and better staff offices; conversion of the old dormitories into

classrooms; new ICT suites; and a splendid, spacious and high-ceilinged art school. The boarding houses and Music Recital Room were new builds, but the remainder were conversions and adaptations in the original core shell. Grade II Building Listing in an area of Outstanding Natural Beauty were undoubtedly constraints but John Franklin's imagination, Estate Bursar Neville Barker's resourceful and practical project management skills, allied to Bursar Tony Waitson's calm and practised eye, enabled a huge amount to be achieved at a reasonable cost. In some respects this was traditional resourceful Woodardian school building but government building regulations allied to an astute Council ensured that unnecessary and dangerous skimping was avoided. It was widely recognised that without the transformation brought about by this upgrading, Ardingly would fall dangerously behind its rivals.

The creative skills of the craftsmen in the maintenance team in these conversions are worth emphasising. A 'can do' approach made the

The School has invested heavily in improving facilities: Working in the new Design Technology Centre and the Library.

The magnificent new Art School.

difference in some complex operations. Over many years, Ardingly has been well served by its support staff, not only craftsmen but also the ground staff, caterers, secretarial and office teams, all of whom come under the umbrella of the Bursar. Responsible for the non-teaching side of school life, their work, often unseen, has been important in providing the infrastructure in which teaching and learning can take place. Many have given a lifetime of service to the School.

Franklin also subtly and sometimes with necessary firmness gradually changed the ethos and culture of the School. The new boarding houses were designed so that house staff and their families could live adjacent to the house and could therefore properly supervise the young in their charge. A less sporting and more academic environment was created. The end of Saturday school in 2004 was indicative of a profound shift in fundamentals. For the first 140 of its 150-year existence Ardingly was a boarding school. Day boys had been introduced for the first time in 1967, but now day pupils constituted

45% of the Senior School student body, all of the Pre-Prep and practically all of the Junior School.

In an age that was putting increasing emphasis on league tables as a means of comparing schools, Franklin appreciated the need to raise Ardingly's academic profile.

League tables have been much criticised by educationalists. The measurement of a school by public exam results is crude. But like it or not, public measurement and accountability were here to stay.

Top left: A study bedroom in Mertens House.
Top right: Common room at Woodlands.
Bottom left: Socialising on The Burse.
Bottom right: Common room at Crosse House.

Junior Athletics.

Recorder lesson in the Pre-Prep.

Junior School pupils.

Prospective parents studied meticulously the tables produced by the national press. Schools took notice. They put more emphasis on the quality of learning in the classroom and were less tolerant of inadequate teaching. These tables made no reference however to the value added in academic performance, nor to the wider value of an independent school education — development of character, leadership, the ability to work in teams and resilience, for example — which the Ardingly parents so much appreciate.

Another external factor affecting academic life was inspection. The government's determination to raise standards had led to OFSTED and the requirement that independent schools also be formally inspected in a systematic way. Both Senior and Junior Schools at Ardingly therefore found themselves inspected regularly. The effect of this was to raise standards, bring in new ideas from other schools, and in some senses to standardise. A uniformity began to emerge in independent schools. On one level this was disadvantageous in taking away individuality. On the other hand, it led to best practice being widely disseminated.

An exciting and imaginative move was the introduction in 2001 of the International Baccalaureate as an alternative to the A Level

programme in the Sixth Form. Since it offers a broader programme of academic study in which six, rather than four, subjects are studied the IB is also attractive to European and especially German students. It is a worldwide course embracing a strong ideal of service, bringing together race and creed and fostering ideals of tolerance and global harmony. It has made the School different from its rivals and helped to boost boarding numbers.

At the end of the day however it is the intellectual calibre and capacities of the pupils allied to the commitment of the teachers in the classroom that are the most important factors in any school's academic performance. Ardingly has been well served by its teachers. Many have devoted the major part of their careers — indeed lives — to the School. The intake of 1951 has already been mentioned. Christopher Bulteel made some very good appointments, including several who served for many years, including Geoffrey Boxall (history 1962–99), George Robb (English and football 1964–86), Tom King (classics 1965–2002), John Baker (modern languages 1966–2000) and Martyn Hodgson (biology 1967–91). Hugely dedicated, they have been at the heart of all that has been accomplished in the past 40 years and follow in the long tradition

May Ball, 2007.

established by the likes of Hilton and Lewington. Others came in for short periods, proved themselves and then moved on to promotion and wider experiences. Both John Franklin's external appointments as Deputy Head were appointed to headships, Mark Eagers (1999–2003) and Michael Carslaw (2003–08), the former to Box Hill School in Surrey, the latter to St Leonard's School, St Andrews in Scotland. Successive heads of the Junior School, Julie Robinson (1999–2003) and Mark Groome (2003–07) were promoted to lead independent preparatory schools, the former to Vinehall at Robertsbridge, the latter to Prestfelde, a Woodard school in Shrewsbury. It is great credit to Ardingly that its senior people are considered so highly in the world of independent schools.

In the summer of 2007, John Franklin left after nine years to become the Headmaster of Christ's Hospital, the first Ardingly head to move on to another headship since Pearson in 1914. Forward-looking, bold and resolute, he had taken every opportunity to modernise the School and the outlook

of Ardingly had been transformed as a result: pupil numbers had risen, the league table position improved (not least with the help of the IB students), and the finances had been notably strengthened.

To take the School into its 150th year and beyond, the Council appointed 42-year-old Peter

Peter Green, seen here with students, succeeded John Franklin as Headmaster in Autumn 2007.

ARDINGLY IN AFRICA

Making a difference . . .

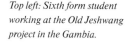

Top left: Sixth form student working at the Old Jeshwang project in the Gambia.

Far right: The School has raised funds through the Langalanga project to sponsor children at school in Kenya. In 2007 they launched an appeal to raise money to build a primary school in Kenya.

Bottom left: Duke of Edinburgh training in Buxton.

Green. A Scot, he had been educated at St Joseph's College, Dumfries, and Edinburgh University where he read geography. He had wide teaching and pastoral experience in boarding schools with spells at Strathallan, Uppingham and Ampleforth where he had been Deputy Head for five years. A man with vision and drive, he was ideally qualified to become Ardingly's eleventh Headmaster, and to develop further the Woodardian heritage, moulded and shaped by his ten predecessors.

What indeed would the Founder, Nathaniel Woodard make of it all if by some heavenly wizardry of modern technology he could be sent the most recent copy of the *Annals* (2006) as Ardingly sets out on its 150th year? He would be staggered to read of the

volume and range of activities — vibrant and creative art; absorbing plays; abundant music both classical and contemporary; expeditions galore — design and technology fieldwork in Wales, artists to New York, one group of historians to Cracow, another to the First World War battlefields, CCF Adventurous Training in the Bavarian Alps, a pre-season football training camp in Valencia, a school expedition to Gambia, and Ardinians on a World Challenge Expedition to Peru. Undoubtedly, he would have been perplexed by the religious studies visit to a Thai Buddhist temple in Wimbledon, though touched that all of Shell was taken to see the original school building in Shoreham and indeed to visit his tomb at Lancing. Exciting outdoor pursuits, conferences and gatherings various, a May

Ball, an Upper Sixth Leavers' Dinner with a list of those (most of them) going to university, a huge and varied amount of sport for boys and girls, including one cricketer, Ben Brown, stepping out in the footsteps of George Brann, Billy Newham, Paul Phillipson and Toby Peirce to play for Sussex. Undoubtedly, too, he would have noted the photos of the pupils, smiling confidently, feeling at ease in what they were about.

All of this reflects a modern, successful and creative 21st-century school — a community with many and varied opportunities for young people. It is a very far cry from Victorian Ardingly with its cramped and primitive accommodation; barely adequate food; a basic curriculum taught by well-meaning but often under-educated and unqualified teachers; very limited facilities for both educational and leisure activities; discipline enforced by the rod, often indiscriminately used; and the year divided up into two long halves.

There are two other features which appear in the *Annals* and which, although less obvious, would please Woodard and suggest to him that his ideals have not been forgotten. The Chaplain's Report is to be found as the first item in the 2006 *Annals*. Clearly the Chapel and Crypt are alive and well and also important in the life of the community. But what does it mean to be a Christian school in a very different world from that in which it was

Students have a wide range of opportunities; both in educational and leisure activities.

OA Veterans' reunion, 2006.

founded? The Chaplain, Fr Ian Colson, writes in his report:

'... for me the concepts of gentleness, openness, a rigour of thought balanced with the witnesses of scripture and tradition and a firm belief that the Church is not about exclusion but inclusion are profoundly appropriate for us as a school. They give us the basis by which we can honour and respect our students, allowing them to find space and time to ask the big questions and to make their answers their own.'

Secondly, Woodard would delight in the physical setting seen in the photographs of school activities. He had an eye for location and the spaciousness and beauty of Ardingly's 250 acres are evident. The unrivalled view from the Terrace is untarnished, and so, too, is that from Nine Acre back to the main school buildings, silhouetted against the skyline. The woods, the lakes and the extensive playing fields are as delightful a setting for a school as can be imagined.

The School was founded with a particular view in mind – a view spiritual and a view physical. How pleased and proud the Founder and all Ardinians can be that both are alive and well 150 years later.

Twenty Old Ardinians

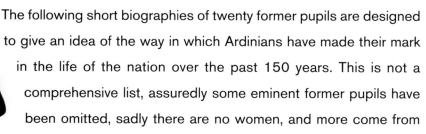

The following short biographies of twenty former pupils are designed to give an idea of the way in which Ardinians have made their mark in the life of the nation over the past 150 years. This is not a comprehensive list, assuredly some eminent former pupils have been omitted, sadly there are no women, and more come from the last 50 rather than the first 100 years of the School's life.

Service to society, locally and nationally and in countless different ways, has been one of Ardingly's distinguishing hallmarks. Many Ardinians have, of course, made immense contributions — in medicine, as teachers, in the City, in business, for example — and are widely regarded in their own communities. The people listed here are some of those whose names might be, or have been, known by a wider public.

The Most Reverend Doctor Walter Adams (C 1885 –93) – Archbishop of British Columbia. In the School's first one hundred years when Britain still had an empire, the *Annals* records many former pupils going out to all corners of the globe to serve and make their life's work as farmers, traders, bankers, administrators and missionaries, '*chaps who went out to Boerland and Zululand and Burma and Cyprus and Hong Kong and lived and died as officers and gentlemen*', as described by Kipling.

Born in 1877, he spent eight years at Ardingly before going on to Hurstpierpoint for the Sixth Form. He studied at Durham University, where he was President of Boats, and was ordained as a priest in 1902. Curacies in County Durham and Lambeth were followed by five years as a missionary priest in Saskatchewan, Canada. Returning to this country, he served for ten years in London as a lecturer in a training college and then Diocesan Inspector of Schools in Southwark. He also found time to be Secretary and then President of the Old Ardinians Society. In 1925, he returned to Canada where he

A competitor in the annual Senior School steeplechase, 2007.

served for the rest of his career as a bishop in three separate dioceses (Caribou, Kootenay and Yukon) and also as Archbishop of British Columbia. He died in 1957.

Sir Andrew Bowden (G 1943–46) – Member of Parliament. '*Bowden you're a leader in this school - the leader of the troublemakers*', so said George Snow when he encountered the 16 year old Andrew Bowden one day in the Cloisters. Given that it is one of the prime jobs of parliament to check the government, this was no bad endorsement!

Born in 1930, Bowden is candid about his lack of academic progress at Ardingly: '*I just worked at the things that interested me and was idle the rest of the time*'. His experiences however were not wasted: '*I am still glad that I used to get a particular form of punishment .... word cards with hundreds of words on them. You had to choose twenty or thirty words, write them out separately and add the dictionary definition against them. You took these to the master and he would ask you to define about five. If you had more than two wrong you got another five. I did not realise at the time how much I learnt in this way.*' His warmth of personality and approachability did however shine through at Ardingly, and again these were valuable characteristics in a political life.

On leaving school he worked in industry and then in personnel. Cutting his teeth as a member of Wandsworth Borough Council, he stood in three General Elections before being elected as Conservative MP for Brighton Kemptown in 1970.

He was to be an assiduous constituency representative and active backbencher for 27 years, serving on several Select Committees, before losing his seat in the Labour landslide of 1997. Coincidentally, Ardingly's other MP of recent times, Sir John Gorst (E 1942-46), served in the House for exactly the same period as Member for Hendon North. Both Bowden and Gorst were knighted in 1994.

For ten years Bowden was National Chairman of the Young Conservatives. He also served as a member of the Chichester Diocesan Synod and for fifteen years as a member of the Ardingly Council. Snow might have been surprised by this but in fact Bowden rendered great service to the School in this way, an entrée into, and direct link with, the world of Westminster is always useful for an independent school.

George Brann (B 1876–87) – Sussex cricketer and England footballer. Ardingly's most notable sportsman was born in 1865 and spent eight years playing for the Ardingly XI as a pupil 1878–83, and as a probationary teacher 1884–86. He was an outstanding Sussex cricketer from 1883 to 1905, scoring runs consistently and often when they were most needed for an average of 26.55 and including 24 centuries. In 1892 he scored two centuries in the

George Brann.

match v Kent at Hove; until then only W.G. Grace had achieved this feat.

He went on three tours under the English flag, to Australia 1887–88, South Africa 1891 and USA 1899, and although he scored centuries in each country, never actually played in a Test match.

He played football for Corinthians, Sussex and on two occasions, England. He is still the only Ardinian to have gained a full international cap for football or cricket.

After retirement he took up golf and led a team to South Africa in 1930. He died in 1954.

Sir Bill Cotton (C 1937– 46) – television producer and executive: Managing, Director BBC Television 1981–87. The son of legendary bandleader Billy Cotton, he was born in 1928. At Ardingly the *Annals* records his involvement in debating, acting and in command of the CCF Band, though he was never especially successful academically.

Starting out in the music business, he joined the BBC in 1956 as an in-house producer of light entertainment programmes, including the *Billy Cotton Band Show* and the *Six-Five Special*. In 1970 he was promoted to Head of Light Entertainment and oversaw a whole series of highly popular comedy programmes such as *Monty Python's Flying Circus*, *The Two Ronnies*, and *Morecambe and Wise*. These all became iconic parts of British culture and this era is generally seen as the most popular in the history of BBC light entertainment. In 1977 he became the Controller of BBC One, the Corporation's prime and the UK's oldest, television station. Then in 1981 he became Managing Director of Television and remained in that post till his retirement in 1987.

He was a hugely influential figure in the nation's broadcasting and helped significantly in creating the success of the BBC in this period. His knighthood for services to television was well earned and his autobiography 'Double Bill: 80 Years of Entertainment' was published in 2000.

Charles Crufts (1868–76) – Founder of the eponymous dog show. To most people Crufts means simply the most famous dog show in the world, held each March nowadays at the National Exhibition Centre in Birmingham. The 2007 Show, for example, attracted 150,000 visitors and huge media coverage.

Charles Crufts.

It has become part of the nation's culture. But where does it all come from?

Charles Crufts went to St Saviour's at Shoreham in 1868, moved with it to Ardingly and left the College in 1876 determined not to enter the family jewellery business. Instead, he joined the dog biscuit manufacturer James Spratt, rising to the post of General Manager. He travelled to dog shows in the UK and abroad, established contacts and came to appreciate the need for higher standards. In 1891 he founded his own show, 'Crufts Greatest Dog Show' at the Royal Agricultural Hall, Islington. It was for all breeds and there were 2,500 entries in the first year. It was held annually and with increasing popularity until his death in 1938. In due course his widow sold it to the Kennel Club who have run it ever since.

Charles Crufts is buried in Highgate Cemetery. The institution he founded is renowned throughout the world but very few people know of its founder's Ardingly origins.

John Delafons (JH, D 1942–49) – Civil Servant and planner. Born in 1930 and brought up by his mother who had separated from his father. She scraped together just enough money to enable him to attend Ardingly on a scholarship where he had an

outstanding career, culminating in the post of Head Boy. He took a first in English at St Peter's, Oxford and joined the civil service in 1953. Subsequently, he was a Harkness Scholar at both Harvard and MIT.

He was Private Secretary to Richard Crossman when the latter became Minister for Housing and Local Government, and received a very good chit in Crossman's 'Diaries of a Cabinet Minister, 1964-70'. For example, *'(John Delafons) is proving a magnificent Private Secretary, devoted, enthusiastic and .... enormously helpful.'* He rose steadily, ultimately to the post of Deputy Secretary at the Department of the Environment. The well known historian Professor Peter Hennessy who knew him for 40 years wrote: *'JD spoke truth unto power. This is probably why he didn't become a Permanent Secretary. He told Ministers what they needed to know, rather than what they wanted to hear.'*

His expertise was in planning and land use and he wrote several important books on the subject, incorporating his experiences of the USA. From 1993 to 2001 he was a Visiting Professor in the Department of Land Management and Development at Reading University. He was married with four daughters and died in 2007.

Mike Hawthorn (G 1942–46) – World Champion Motor Racing Driver. The most glamorous Old Ardinian and in his day a household name. Born in 1929, his father, a veteran Brooklands man, owned and ran the Tourist Trophy Garage in Farnham. Racing was in Mike's blood. 'Snowball' as he was known at school in view of his striking shock of very blond hair was a first-class shot, played the bugle in the CCF Band and specialised in illicit trips to the cinemas and fleshpots of Haywards Heath. Studying was less enticing and he left school before taking the Higher School Certificate. His last night at Ardingly was marked by the spectacular racing of an Austin 7 (not his own) around the playing fields.

He attended the Chelsea Automobile Engineering Training College, before going to work for his father. Increasingly, however, competitive motor racing came to rule his life. By 1952, he had become one of the two foremost British drivers (Stirling Moss was the other), serving with BRM and then with Jaguar. In only his second season he became the first British driver since 1932 to win a

Grand Prix. He was appointed then as chief driver to Ferrari. It was in October 1958, following the Moroccan Grand Prix, that he became the World Champion Motor Racing Driver and a national hero. He retired whilst at the very top.

He had always lived life to the full both on and off the track and, according to the inquest, it was speed in treacherous weather conditions which led to his tragic death in an accident on the Guildford by-pass on 22nd January 1959 just a few months after his supreme triumph.

Sir Claude Hayes (E 1924–30) – Civil Servant . If ever there was a tale to warm the heart of Nathaniel Woodard and to illustrate the possibility of upward mobility for young people of ability from less privileged backgrounds, it was Claude Hayes.

Born in 1912, a local village carpenter's son, he passed the 11+ at elementary school, and the County Education Committee paid for him to attend Ardingly as a day boy. Enjoying the challenge of learning new subjects such as French, Latin and chemistry, he did very well academically but found that most boys left at 16 to go into banks or the services, and that there was little Sixth Form education. Fortuitously, he was taught and inspired by George Coghlin who prepared him for entry to his old college at Oxford, St Edmund Hall, and also ensured that there was financial support from the Ardingly College Scholarship Fund. Hayes proved to be an outstanding undergraduate, and after further study at the Sorbonne, returned to Oxford as a don.

In due course he joined the Civil Service and after war service in the army, rose steadily through the ranks of the Treasury, helping in particular in the unwinding of the Central African Federation, and later the West Indies Federation. His last post was as Chairman of the Crown Agents for Overseas Governments and Administration.

John Hayes, CBE (C 1942–49) – leading authority on Gainsborough and Director of the National Portrait Gallery 1974-94. Born in London in 1929, he had a successful Ardingly career, read history at Keble College, Oxford, and then undertook postgraduate study at the Courtauld Institute.

His professional life encompassed 20 years each in two national institutions. From 1954, he was assistant keeper and from 1970, Director of the London Museum, crucially leading its transfer from a wing of Kensington Palace to its new home in the Barbican as the Museum of London. His imaginative approach to the concept of this museum, allied to his adroit management of colleagues, Whitehall and politicians, helped him to be appointed to the important post of director of the National Portrait Gallery in 1974. For the next 20 years he developed this world-renowned institution, orchestrating the Orange Street extension, commissioning new portraits, for example, that by Bryan Organ of Diana, Princess of Wales, raising funds, undertaking initiatives such as the 'acceptance in lieu' scheme to retain paintings in their historic setting.

Immensely hard working and committed, he was able to produce a number of publications, not least on the 18th century painter Thomas Gainsborough, on whom he was one of the leading authorities.

He died in 2006. His younger brother, Peter, taught in the Junior School from 1971 to 1996.

Ian Hislop (JH, A 1968–77) – satirical writer and broadcaster: Editor of *Private Eye* since 1985, and a Team Captain on *Have I Got News for You* since 1990.

Currently, he is the most widely known Ardinian. Born in 1959, brought up abroad, his father died when he was 13, so that Ardingly came to play a very big part in his life. He began acting in the Junior School under the direction of Roger Grove Smith, not least as the harassed headmaster, Mr Pond in *The Happiest Days of Your Life*: '*the authority of a headmaster seemed to come quite naturally to him*', said The Junior School magazine, *The Martlet*. In the Senior School he found Colin Temblett-Wood an especially stimulating and thought-provoking teacher. He was a distinguished Head of School.

He went up to Magdalen College, Oxford where he read English.

'At Oxford I ran a magazine called Passing Wind ... And most of the main contributors were Old Ardinians. In fact, a lot of the things I have done since leaving I've done with people I met at Ardingly. Anyway, that was my introduction to journalism and then came Private Eye *and television.'*

Ian Hislop.

played or conducted premieres, organ recitals and broadcasts throughout the world.

Some outstanding teachers helped to inspire him and to foster his varied talents — his tutor, Chris Potter, Bob Hemingway and Tom King in the classics, John Craig in English, and Alan Angus, Victor Bradley, Martin Cannings and Michael Bigg in the Music department. Ardingly helped him to see that in a career as a cathedral organist, he needed to take a wider view than the narrowly musical. The first sight of the dormitory with 20 beds on each side, compulsory games and the CCF, were less appealing but, in retrospect, gave opportunities he would not otherwise have had.

'And, surrounding all this, the wonderful Sussex countryside, and the incomparable view from the Terrace. Sitting in the organ loft in January 2000 during CHB's Memorial Service and looking down the Chapel, bathed in the gentle sunlight of a winter's morning, the years fell away .... But the memories are as strong as ever, and the consciousness of debt to the institution and to so many individuals, both fellow-pupils and staff — too many of them no longer with us - is more and more real with the passing years.'

He describes satire as 'the bringing to ridicule of vice, folly and humbug', claims to be the most sued man in English legal history and has appeared in every episode of *Have I Got News for You*, in its 17 year history. From time to time he has involved himself in serious work, presenting Channel 4 television programmes on the First World War and on the relationship between education and the church, for example.

James Lancelot (A 1966–70) — Master of the Choristers and Organist, Durham Cathedral since 1985. Ardingly's exceptional music has seeped into the souls of countless pupils laying at a formative age the foundations of an interest and love for life. A very few have been able to make it their life's work and James Lancelot is one of Ardingly's most distinguished musicians.

Born in 1952, he came to Ardingly from St Paul's Cathedral Choir School and subsequently studied at the Royal College of Music and at King's College, Cambridge where he was the Organ Scholar, before setting out on his professional career — Assistant Organist at St Clement Danes and Hampstead Parish Church 1974–75, Sub-Organist at Winchester Cathedral 1975–85, and then to one of the leading positions in the land as Master of the Choristers and Organist at Durham Cathedral. He is one of Britain's best known church musicians and has

Sir Robin McLaren (C 1949–51) — diplomat: Ambassador to China 1991–94. He arrived halfway through the summer term of 1949 with no previous experience of boarding. As he settled down, he began to benefit from the great range of things on offer in the Snow era, joining a variety of clubs and societies, as well as the choir and orchestra. He had the good fortune to be taught history by Michael Watts and he won a scholarship to St. John's College, Cambridge.

National Service in the Royal Navy came first, and then after graduation he joined the Foreign Office in 1985. He was selected to specialise in Chinese and rose steadily with postings to Hong Kong, Peking, Rome and Copenhagen, before serving as Ambassador to the Philippines from 1985–87.

From 1991 to 1994 he was a notable Ambassador to China at a crucial stage as this country was opening up to the rest of the world and also involved in tense and significant negotiations with Britain over the future of Hong Kong. Sir Robin's sure touch and capacity to understand and work with China's leaders served Britain well.

As a retired ambassador, he has been in big demand in a number of charitable and educational activities, not least as a wise and far seeing member of the School Council and its Chairman from 1999 to 2005.

Sir David Manning (C 1962–66) – diplomat: Ambassador to the USA 2003–07. It is remarkable how many Old Ardinians have held very senior diplomatic posts during the last 20 years. Sir Robin McLaren (C 1949–51), Ambassador to the Philippines and then China 1991–94; Ian Mackley (C 1953–61), High Commissioner to Ghana 1996-2000; A.M. Wood (C 1953–57), Ambassador to Yugoslavia; Sir Edward Jackson (C 1922–24), Ambassador to Belgium; and Robert Alston (A 1949–56), Ambassador to Oman and High Commissioner to New Zealand 1994–98, and also incidentally the current and highly esteemed Chairman of the School Council.

A Scholar at Ardingly, Sir David read modern history at Oriel College, Oxford,before studying at the John Hopkins University School of Advanced International Studies. He joined the Foreign Office in 1972 and after early postings in Warsaw, New Delhi and Paris, had his first senior position in Moscow. Spells in Whitehall and representing the UK on the Conference on the former Yugoslavia in 1994, were a prelude to his ambassadorship to Israel 1995–98.

The next five years were spent in London, and he was pivotal in Prime Minister Blair's Downing Street in the period post 9/11 – advising on the conflict in Iraq, guiding relations with President Bush, dealing with the Israelis, the Arab governments, the Russians, and the Chinese. One national newspaper described him thus: 'He is an old fashioned public servant – nothing flashy, assiduous, polite, and extremely modest.'

In 2003 he was appointed to Washington, the highest ranking British diplomatic posting. He is the most eminent Old Ardinian.

The Right Reverend Gordon Mursell (D 1962–66) – Bishop of Stafford from 2005. Given Ardingly's strong Christian dimension it is no surprise that a number of former pupils have found their vocation in the Anglican priesthood.

Born in 1949, he came to the School on the recommendation of a family friend, Reverend John Neal, the former Chaplain. He won an Exhibition in History to Brasenose College, Oxford and was ordained priest in 1974. He has had a rich and varied career in the Church of England. Curate in Walton, Liverpool, ten years as Vicar in a busy urban parish, St John's, East Dulwich, a tutor at Salisbury & Wells Theological College, Team Rector in Stafford, and then Provost (later Dean) of Birmingham 1999-2005, before being appointed Bishop of Stafford in 2005. He has also found the time to write several theological books.

Looking back, he feels he owes much to Ardingly. A wise tutor and classics teacher, Bob Hemingway, who made him feel that he mattered when he arrived at the School with his confidence at a low ebb. Its music and, in particular, a teacher, Victor Bradley, who imparted the keyboard skills and intellectual rigour needed to accompany an innate love of music. Its sport, not in organised team games but rather in discovering he had a capacity for long distance running which in due course led on to a passion for the Munros of Scotland. And, most of all, a sensitive housemaster, David Harris, who supported him and his brother when as teenagers their father died unexpectedly.

Billy Newham (1881–87) – Sussex Cricketer. Many of cricket's historic roots lie in Sussex. The professional game and the County Championship became established in the latter part of the 19th century and Sussex has always been one of the foremost county teams. Billy Newham devoted himself to its cause for 63 years from his debut as an 18 year old in 1881 to his death aged 81 in 1944, as player, Captain, Secretary and Assistant Secretary.

As a pupil, then as a pupil teacher, he was a highly successful member of the Ardingly XI in the early 1880s. One of the mainstays of the Sussex batting, he was an attractive batsman with a wide variety of strokes and a wonderfully quick eye. His cutting of the fast bowlers was merciless. He was a magnificent outfielder.

Extremely handsome with dark, wavy hair and a well tended moustache, he toured Australia with Arthur Shrewsbury's side in 1887, but sadly accomplished little. He was Captain of Sussex in 1889 and again 1891–92. In 1902, at the age of 42, he set a new world record with a stand of 344 for the seventh wicket with Ranji against Essex at Leytonstone. In all he scored 14,554 runs at an average of 25.62 and took ten wickets at 62.80 each.

He was a dedicated Secretary of the County Club for 20 years, and then helped out as Assistant Secretary during the Second World War till he died in office.

Paul Reynolds (E 1959–63) – BBC diplomatic correspondent. In a global economy and society modern communications mean that news is instant. To have journalists based throughout the World who can report and commentate authoritatively and with immediacy is both reassuring and necessary. Paul Reynolds has been an outstanding BBC correspondent for the past 40 years from New York, Jerusalem, Brussels and New York again. His clear and coherent reporting of events and placing them in context have been familiar to all listeners to Radio 4.

Born in 1946, he came to Ardingly from a prep school in Seaford on an Exhibition, had a successful school career before going on to Worcester College, Oxford to read history. Two years as a cub reporter on the *Eastern Daily Press* was a basis for his career with the BBC.

His son, James, has followed the family tradition and is now the BBC's correspondent in Beijing.

Victor Silvester (1911–14) – bandleader whose dance band sound was the best known in the world. Born in 1900, he was brought up in a strict Victorian vicarage, his father being Vicar of St John the Evangelist, Wembley. Attracted by the low fees and the High Anglicanism of Ardingly, he went off to boarding school aged 11, and ran away aged 14 years and 9 months in 1914 to join the army, claiming to be 18. He was wounded in the trenches, and ended the War as a stretcher-bearer in northern Italy, where he was awarded the Italian Al Valore Military Bronze Medal.

He studied music at Trinity College but soon became totally hooked on dancing techniques, winning the World Professional Dancing Championship title in 1922. Together with his wife, an excellent dancer and former Beauty Queen, they

established the Victor Silvester Dance Academy in Bond Street. His book *Modern Ballroom Dancing* became the definitive rule book for dancing and sold in millions.

Dance competitions were held all over the country, and he formed a 'Strict Tempo' orchestra and made his broadcasting debut in 1937. His trademark catchphrase was 'Slow, Slow, Quick, Quick, Slow'. Over the next four decades his records sold more than 75 million throughout the world. He adapted to Jive, which arrived with the American forces in World War II, and produced a number of records for this new craze.

In his lifetime, he made over 6,500 radio and TV broadcasts. He was featured in *This Is Your Life* in 1958, and awarded the OBE for services to ballroom dancing in 1961.

He died in 1978. Music and dancing were his life's work and he had a profound effect on ballroom dancing, leaving a legacy of 'how it should be done', right through to the present day.

Victor Silvester, dancing with his wife.

T.T.H. Stevens (Terry-Thomas) (A 1924–28) – Character actor. Born in 1911, he attended prep school in Finchley, being sent to Ardingly aged 13. He had no great academic accomplishments but was stimulated by the beautiful surroundings and mellow buildings. He came into his own when he formed a jazz band, named the Rhythm Maniacs. Consisting of ukulele (played by him), piano and banjo, and playing at school functions in the Under. Soon he realised that he had the capacity to entertain people. Much later in life he wrote: *'The satisfaction I got when I made people laugh was indescribably potent.'*

Leaving school aged 17 in 1928, he joined his father in Smithfield Market as a fifteen shillings a week transport clerk. It was not, however, till the 1930s that his acting career began to take off, and then came the War when he served in the Royal Corps of Signals. Returning to civilian life he became one of the best known characters on the British cinema screen. He was the extra-special English cad whose meticulous moustache, crisp and suave upper-class accent, dapper dress and impeccable manners supported the charm which was used in all manner of nefarious adventures. He appeared in more than 50 films including *Lucky Jim, I'm All Right Jack, School for Scoundrels, Monte Carlo or Bust!* and *Those Magnificent Men In Their Flying Machines.*

His later years were affected by Parkinson's disease although his autobiography, *Terry-Thomas Tells Tales*, was published just before he died in 1990.

Sir Robert Tasker (G 1882–84) – Member of Parliament and Chairman of London County Council 1930–31. Service to the community is an Ardingly hallmark. In his profession as an architect, his involvement in the Territorial Army and in both national and London politics, Robert Tasker played a significant role in British life in the first half of the 20th century. Born in 1868, he was at Ardingly for two years in the 1880s. Articled to his father's architectural practice, he became Senior Partner in 1916. Later, he was to play a notable role in the governance of his profession serving as a member of RIBA and for 14 years a member of the Council of Architects Registration Council of UK.

His life though was not confined to architecture. From 1885 to 1920 he served in the Volunteers and

Adam Virgo playing for Brighton and Hove Albion against Wolves, 2004.

Territorial Forces, and raised and commanded a battalion of the London Regiment in 1915.

He was a member of the London County Council from 1910 to 1937, serving as Chairman in 1930-31. On the right-wing of the Conservative Party, he represented East Islington in the House of Commons 1924–29, and Holborn 1933–45. He was knighted in 1931.

Active until the end of his long life, he had always taken an interest in his old school, served as President of the OA Society in 1922–23 and was present at the Centenary celebrations just a few months before he died.

Adam Virgo (GH 1996–2000) – footballer. Ardingly's football has always been strong. Golden ages were the 1880s and then the 1990s when a host of excellent players were attracted to the School by Sporting Awards. Six appearances in the Independent Schools Cup Final with a win in 1998, and victory in the English Schools Cup in 1999, were symbols of these successes. Following the 1999 winning of the cup, The Times indeed said that Ardingly was the strongest independent school team there had ever been.

Adam Virgo is the best known of some outstanding players at the School in this period. "There has not been a more effective player at Ardingly and his dominance will be sadly missed," said the Annals when he left the School, aged 17, to join Brighton and Hove Albion. A strong and resolute defender, he established himself as a fine player in the First Division, being their player of the season in 2004-05. Thereupon he was transferred to Glasgow Celtic for £1 million. Injuries have subsequently impaired his progress and he has had spells on loan to Coventry City and Colchester United.

Chairmen, Heads and Bursars

Chairman of the College Council

1926–42	Canon R.J. Lea
1942–46	Colonel J.R. Warren
1947–50	Major General R.M. Luckock
1950–51	Captain G.H. Warner, DSC, RN
1951	M.R. Lubbock
1952–63	J.R.W. Alexander, CBE
1964–72	The Venerable G. Mayfield
1972–94	M.R. Toynbee, JP
1994–99	Lady Anne Thorne
1999–2005	Sir Robin McLaren
2005–	R.J. Alston

Headmasters

1858–94	Revd. F.M.D. Mertens
1894–1904	Revd. F.K. Hilton
1904–11	Revd. H.A. Rhodes
1911–14	Revd. M. Pearson
1915–32	Revd. T.E. Wilson
1933–46	Revd. E.C. Crosse
1947–61	Revd. G.d'O. Snow
1962–80	C.H. Bulteel
1980–98	J.W. Flecker
1998–2007	J.R. Franklin
2007–	P.R.A. Green

Second Master / Deputy Head

1939–60	H.H. Herring
1960–66	H.R. Miller
1967–81	D.G. Knight
1981–99	M.G. Cannings
1999–2003	M. Eagers
2003–08	M.J.H. Carslaw

Master / Head of the Junior School

1912–27	G.H.G. Nicholson
1928–35	G.C. Miller
1936–49	E.A. Winnington-Ingram
1950–54	M.L.B. Hall
1954–67	A.D. Ellis
1967–86	R. Grove Smith
1986–95	Revd. R.P. Marsh
1995–96	P. Thwaites
1996–98	Revd. J. Spencer
1999–2002	Mrs J. Robinson
2002–07	M. Groome
2007–	C. Calvey

Head of Pre-Prep and Farmhouse

1992–2006	Mrs S.M. Vermeer
2007–	Ms J.L. Adkins

Bursars

1935–48	J.F.B. Wardale
1948–52	Brigadier W.O. Lay
1953–65	Air Commodore G.P.H. Carter
1965–69	Major General R.C.H. Leathes
1969–83	Wing Commander E.R. Dutt
1983–96	Group Captain J.M. Lewendon
1996–	A.R. Waitson

The view from the Chapel tower.

APPENDIX C

School Register, January 2008

Surname	Year		
B. Abbaszadeh	Upper Sixth	E.G. Bayne	Year 4
K.N. Abery	Year 8	R.M. Beaven	Year 4
L.G. Adamson	Year 3	T.P. Beaven	Year 7
A.D. Agyeman-Duah	Upper Sixth	J. Beer	Remove
L.E. Akinwunmi	Year 8	M.D. Beer	Upper Sixth
C.D. Allery	Upper Sixth	C.J. Bell	Remove
O.R. Altman	Year 7	F.K. Bell	Remove
S.A. Altman	Remove	H.E. Bell	Year 8
T.J. Altman	Lower Sixth	H.M. Bell	Year 4
R.G.P. Amos	Lower Sixth	O.F. Bell	Remove
J.C. Anderson	Fifth	T.A. Bell	Year 6
T.S. Anderson	Shell	M.A. Bennett	Year 7
T.E. Andrews	Year 7	H. Berry	Year 8
Z.Z. Andrews	Year 6	A.M. Best	Fifth
A.G. Angelova	Fifth	C. Biglia	Lower Sixth
I.R. Anson	Nursery	C.A. Bischoff	Fifth
T. Anson	Year 3	J.A. Bishop	Year 6
T.F.B. Ashwell	Fifth	J.P. Bishop	Year 4
C.M.S. Austin	Lower Sixth	J.S. Bishop	Year 1
A.J. Awang	Remove	J.R. Bleach	Fifth
M.O. Awang	Year 7	A.G. Bliss	Shell
J.A. Ayloff	Year 6	L.A.T. Blomfield	Remove
P.C. Ayloff	Shell	C.V.R. Board	Fifth
N. Badger	Year 2	S.K.H. Board	Year 8
O.M. Badger	Year 4	A. Bohills	Lower Sixth
T.P. Badger	Year 7	J.J. Bolton	Upper Sixth
G.Y.V. Baekelandt	Lower Sixth	D. Bone	Year 5
K. Baguma	Lower Sixth	G. Bone	Shell
T.D. Bain	Remove	E.N. Bongards	Lower Sixth
C. Baker	Shell	J.J. Botting	Remove
E.V. Baker	Shell	W.K.J. Bouch	Fifth
O.H. Baker	Year 7	J.L. Bower	Fifth
Z.L.V. Baker	Shell	G.E. Bower-Nye	Year 1
L. Bankovich	Shell	J.A. Bowman	Year 8
G.D. Banks	Fifth	D.L. Boyd	Remove
H.R. Banks	Upper Sixth	T.F. Boyd	Lower Sixth
L. Bansal	Year 1	T.G. Bradbeer	Fifth
J.G. Barber	Shell	W.M. Bradbeer	Lower Sixth
H.C.H. Barker	Year 6	C.V. Bradley	Year 2
A.E. Barker-Danby	Lower Sixth	J.V. Bradley	Year 5
J.C. Barry	Upper Sixth	H.E. Branfoot	Fifth
R.A. Bartlett	Remove	H.L. Brann	Year 7
R.A. Bartlett	Year 7	R.J. Braunwarth	Upper Sixth
H. Batchelor	Remove	W.W. Bridges	Year 8
M.A.L. Baxter	Lower Sixth	A.C.S. Broadley	Year 4
C.H. Bayne	Year 7	R.L. Brook	Remove
		L.K. Brown	Shell

N.M. Bruins	Upper Sixth		M. Conteh	Fifth
J.K. Buhr	Lower Sixth		A.C. Cook	Shell
M.A. Buhre-Niedhardt	Lower Sixth		J.A. Cook	Upper Sixth
B.D.G. Burgess	Nursery		T.G.L. Cook	Fifth
J.M.R. Burgess	Year 4		K.L. Cookney	Upper Sixth
J.E.A. Burgess	Year 1		L.A. Coombs	Lower Sixth
T.L. Burgess	Fifth		O.E. Corbett	Nursery
E.J. Burke	Year 8		A. Cordesmeyer	Upper Sixth
M.C.S. Burke	Year 6		M.H. Cosad	Upper Sixth
B.J.M. Burns	Fifth		T.I. Cosad	Lower Sixth
F.J.C. Burns	Remove		L.W. Costick	Year 6
V. Burns	Year 4		J. Cowan	Remove
G. Buschmann	Upper Sixth		M.R.C. Cowan	Lower Sixth
W.G. Butler Denby	Year 3		A.R. Cowie	Year 3
H.L. Butt	Lower Sixth		A.F. Cowie	Year 5
J.O.P. Butt	Year 6		J.J. Cox	Year 7
V.J. Butt	Year 3		V.S.L. Crawford	Year 6
C. Callow	Shell		A. Cristiani	Upper Sixth
O.M. Calvey	Reception		A.A.H. Cufley	Lower Sixth
H.C.S. Carminati	Remove		J.J. Cufley	Upper Sixth
A.F.K. Carslaw	Year 7		M. Cui	Upper Sixth
E.A.J. Carslaw	Remove		R.A.J. Culshaw	Fifth
O.E.R. Carslaw	Year 4		S. Cunningham	Year 6
H. Caunter	Remove		T.P. Cunningham	Year 2
C.T. Cerullo	Fifth		C. Curnock	Year 4
B.F.C. Challis	Year 8		M.W. Daniel	Shell
B.S.J. Chalmers	Pre-Nursery		J.A. Davidson	Year 6
L. Chan	Lower Sixth		A.E. Davis	Year 1
H.S.J. Chandler	Fifth		R.H.N. Davis	Shell
T.S. Chetse	Lower Sixth		S.R. Davis	Lower Sixth
N. Cheung	Lower Sixth		K. Davison	Reception
D. Cheung	Lower Sixth		E. Davison	Year 3
M.A. Chilton	Fifth		C.J. De Caux	Upper Sixth
M.A. Chisholm	Year 2		T.P. Deatcher	Fifth
C. Choi	Upper Sixth		E.M.E. Deeming	Fifth
A.A. Chowdhury	Fifth		B.L. Deery	Fifth
E.A. Christmas	Year 7		J.F. Deery	Upper Sixth
Z.E.G. Christmas	Fifth		N.J. Delo	Pre-Nursery
G.K.O. Chu	Upper Sixth		A.J. Delve	Fifth
J.J. Clack	Year 4		A. Demetriadi	Year 6
T.P. Clack	Year 2		A.P. Dennis	Year 8
A. Clark	Year 8		X.D. Diedrich	Upper Sixth
H.I. Clark	Year 8		J.J. Dollery	Shell
F.L. Clayson	Year 4		J.E. Donoghue	Remove
G.B. Clutton	Remove		L.S. Donoghue	Lower Sixth
R.D. Clutton	Lower Sixth		R.V. Donoghue	Shell
R.H. Cole	Lower Sixth		F.F. Doubtfire	Year 2
R.J.S. Collinge	Fifth		H.A.F. Doyle	Remove
F.M. Collings	Year 6		D.R. Draper	Shell
C.N. Collins	Year 2		L.A. Duckworth	Upper Sixth
P.F. Colson	Remove		C.J.M. Dumeresque	Lower Sixth
R.L. Colson	Remove		T.T. Durkin	Fifth
R.J. Colson	Upper Sixth		W.J. Durkin	Year 8

S.J. Eagers	Lower Sixth	D.C. Garlick	Lower Sixth
R.G. East	Year 7	R.A. Gibbens	Remove
J.T. Edwards	Nursery	T.C.N. Gibbens	Year 7
C.P.W.H. Elder	Year 3	J.C.G. Gibson	Year 8
S.A.H. Elder	Year 4	B.K. Giddings	Fifth
E. Elgee	Year 7	B.M. Giddings	Year 5
L.M.C. Elgee	Remove	V.R.E. Gielgud	Year 2
C. Elwell-Sutton	Nursery	M.H.M. Girvan	Reception
H.M. Elwell-Sutton	Year 3	N.C.O. Girvan	Nursery
A.F. Elwin	Year 7	C.M.C. Godfrey	Upper Sixth
A.H.G. Elwin	Year 5	T.J. Goma'a	Lower Sixth
J.M. Elwin	Shell	D. Gomez	Shell
S.J. Elwin	Fifth	H.P.H. Goodale	Lower Sixth
C.F.W. Emmerich	Lower Sixth	J.J.H. Gorman	Remove
V.K. Emmett	Lower Sixth	C. Gott	Upper Sixth
A.E. Ertl	Year 3	C.J. Gough	Year 6
F.M. Ertl	Year 5	E.P. Gough	Year 7
B.T.A. Evans	Upper Sixth	V.A. Gough	Year 3
L.R. Evans	Year 5	A. Grachvogel	Pre-Nursery
S.E.J. Evans	Remove	F.A.C. Grachvogel	Year 1
W.J. Evans	Year 6	D.P. Gradon	Fifth
H.R.M. Fairall	Fifth	R.E.J. Gray	Shell
B.T.J. Farmer	Shell	E.J.T. Greaves Smith	Shell
T.J.H. Farmer	Year 6	M.L. Green	Year 6
D. Fielding	Year 3	L.I. Griffin	Lower Sixth
N. Fielding	Reception	A. Groves	Lower Sixth
D. Filmer	Year 8	N.M. Groves	Remove
R. Filmer	Year 6	M. Gruger	Fifth
M.A. Filmer-Cox	Reception	A.L.C. Grust	Lower Sixth
T.P. Finnerty	Year 5	E.L. Guerard	Fifth
J.C. Firth	Nursery	S.R. Guerard	Year 6
R.G. Firth	Year 1	D. Gur	Fifth
A. Fithen	Year 8	J.M. Hagen	Lower Sixth
G.G. Fithen	Year 5	O.B. Hague	Year 7
A. Fitzgerald	Fifth	A.A.E. Haines	Shell
E.R.A. Fitzgerald	Shell	L.A.T. Haines	Year 7
S.S. Fleming	Year 7	J.M. Hall	Shell
J.A.S. Floydd	Year 7	D.F. Hamilton	Fifth
S. Floyer	Upper Sixth	R.A. Hamilton	Upper Sixth
C.R. Forbes	Lower Sixth	E.L. Hanan	Year 4
M. Forbes	Remove	W.P. Hand	Shell
J.M.G. Forster	Lower Sixth	T.A.S. Hardcastle	Lower Sixth
J.S. Fortune	Fifth	P.A.E. Hardman	Lower Sixth
O.R.D. Francis	Pre-Nursery	C.A. Hardwick	Lower Sixth
J.P. Frederick	Lower Sixth	P.G. Hardwick	Year 7
R.H.R. Freeman	Year 8	S.R. Hardwick	Year 8
B.K. French	Year 1	A. Harmsworth	Year 6
T.C. French	Year 5	A. Harrington	Year 8
J. Frost	Shell	W. Harrington	Shell
Z. Frost	Pre-Nursery	A.A. Harris	Year 2
M. Fung	Shell	K.E. Harris	Remove
L. Galelli	Lower Sixth	N.J. Harris	Shell
R. Gallie	Upper Sixth	J. Harrison	Shell

T.D. Harrison	Lower Sixth	A.R. Hyland	Fifth
A.M. Hart	Year 3	F.M.R. Hyland	Shell
S.W. Hart	Nursery	M.T. Imber	Year 1
A.V. Harvey	Year 6	B.F.A. Irving	Lower Sixth
C.P. Harvey	Year 4	D. Irving	Shell
S.P. Harvey	Nursery	N.F. Jackson	Remove
R. Hawkins	Remove	P.G. Jackson Eastwood	Shell
S.J. Haydon	Shell	S.A. James	Year 1
B. Henning	Remove	S.R. James	Nursery
J.C. Hepher	Shell	J.J. Jenkins	Year 7
B. Hewitt	Shell	F.M. Jensen	Reception
N.P. Higgs	Shell	H.R. Jensen	Pre-Nursery
C.S. Higham-Stoianova	Shell	M.T. Jensen	Pre-Nursery
K.L.M. Higham-Stoianova	Fifth	E.S. Johnson	Upper Sixth
T. Hill	Upper Sixth	C.E.G. Jones	Fifth
F. Hills	Year 6	J. Jones	Year 7
L.C. Hindle	Year 6	K. Jones	Year 7
T.C. Hindle	Year 4	R.W.F. Jones	Lower Sixth
A. Hines	Remove	E.S. Joseph	Remove
L. Hines	Year 8	S.O. Joshua	Lower Sixth
J.R. Hinge	Upper Sixth	T. Jung	Upper Sixth
C.V.J. Hirst	Fifth	Y.Z. Kalcheva	Lower Sixth
T.D. Hodgins	Shell	A. Kane	Remove
A.W. Hodson	Year 5	C. Kane	Year 8
J.J. Hodson	Nursery	R.A. Karkia	Lower Sixth
Z.P. Hodson	Year 6	B.C. Kay	Year 6
K.E. Hogg	Shell	C.C. Kay	Shell
L.J. Hogg	Year 4	A.M. Kellas	Upper Sixth
T.L. Hogg	Year 6	A. Kemp	Year 6
J. Holden	Fifth	B.L. Kemp	Lower Sixth
C.M. Holmes	Shell	G.A. Kemp	Shell
M. Holmes	Year 7	L.S. Kemp	Year 8
R.C.E. Holmes	Year 4	H. Key	Fifth
O.L. Homewood	Shell	R.A.J. Key	Remove
J.D.H. Hong	Fifth	B.A. Kidger	Shell
E.R. Houlihan	Upper Sixth	M.J. Kidger	Shell
J.S. Howard	Remove	W.P. Kidger	Upper Sixth
J.E. Howell	Year 7	E.M. Kilby	Fifth
M.H.C. Howes	Remove	I.P.G. King	Reception
J. Howie	Upper Sixth	M.C.N. King	Year 5
C.E.F.E. Hoyal	Year 7	M. King	Year 7
X. Hu	Lower Sixth	S.G. King	Shell
S.K.G. Huerholz	Upper Sixth	W.R. King	Year 4
D.A.J. Hughes	Fifth	L.B. Koe	Upper Sixth
I.G. Hughes	Year 7	M.J. Koren	Lower Sixth
K.J. Hughes	Year 5	J.E.P. Kreule	Shell
B. Hui	Lower Sixth	E. Kuhrt	Remove
D.T. Hunter	Remove	F.S.F. Kwok	Upper Sixth
M.J. Hunter	Year 8	C. Lai	Upper Sixth
L. Hunton	Upper Sixth	C.R. Lai	Remove
L.F. Hutton	Fifth	E.L. Lai	Upper Sixth
W.R. Hutton	Remove	E.C.K. Lai	Upper Sixth
A.L. Hyam	Lower Sixth	W.J. Land-Smith	Remove

S.A. Langdon	Nursery	T.K. Maynard	Year 8
Z.B. Langdon	Year 4	B.M.T. McConnell	Year 6
M.W. Large	Shell	C.M. McConnell	Fifth
L. Lau	Upper Sixth	J.I. McCulloch	Reception
G. Lawrence	Year 8	E.J.P. McGahan	Year 8
G.F.S. Lawrence	Year 6	H.J. McGahan	Upper Sixth
H.A.R. Lawrence	Year 4	J. McGahan	Fifth
J.E.A. Lebrument	Upper Sixth	L.J.P. McGahan	Remove
S.C. Lee	Year 6	J. McPherson	Lower Sixth
S.G. Lee	Year 2	M.A. McPherson	Reception
S.J. Lee	Upper Sixth	P.A. McPherson	Year 2
T.H. Lent	Year 4	T.D. McPherson	Year 5
S. Leung	Lower Sixth	E.T.C. Meagher	Year 8
C.F. Leveaux	Upper Sixth	T.C.N. Mellish	Year 3
D.H. Lewis	Year 2	J.A. Merrion	Remove
J.A. Lewis	Nursery	B.W. Metcalfe	Nursery
J.R. Lewis	Upper Sixth	G.J.R.L. Meyerheim	Upper Sixth
S.L. Lewis	Year 3	D.R. Michau	Fifth
T.J. Lewis	Year 5	M.L. Michau	Year 5
K. Li	Remove	M.A. Michau	Year 7
T.T. Lindsey-Jones	Remove	B.C. Milan	Fifth
O.F. Lloyd-Seetim	Year 4	G.T.M. Miller	Upper Sixth
T.A. Lloyd-Seetim	Year 6	K.A. Mokedi	Fifth
O.M. Loader	Fifth	J.N. Monks	Shell
B.M. Long	Year 3	S.F.M. Monks	Upper Sixth
P. Long	Fifth	M.A.G. Monsell	Year 7
S.J. Long	Reception	R.A. Moore-Williams	Reception
H.M. Lummis	Remove	A.J. Mordecai	Pre-Nursery
A.E. Mackay	Shell	O.J. Mordecai	Year 2
I.G. Mackay	Lower Sixth	D.J.A. Morgan	Year 2
F.C. Mackay Bulger	Year 7	D.L. Morgan	Year 7
C.W. Mackintosh	Year 7	O.G. Morgan	Year 8
G.T. Makamure	Remove	K.E. Morrison	Upper Sixth
B. Makazhanov	Upper Sixth	S.A. Mulhall	Remove
O.C.J. Mallett	Reception	K.M. Mulligan	Year 5
J.P. Man	Year 7	E.L. Munday	Shell
M.G. Man	Year 6	T.P. Munday	Shell
T.D.F. Manley	Year 2	A.V. Murch	Fifth
Z.E. Manning	Fifth	M.E. Murphy	Upper Sixth
B.J. Markowski	Year 5	T. Musgrave	Upper Sixth
E.R. Markowski	Year 8	E.A. Newman	Year 4
C.G.B. Marriott	Shell	L.C. Newman	Year 2
C.J. Marsh	Fifth	B.W. Newton	Year 8
M.S. Marsh	Upper Sixth	J.L. Newton	Year 5
J.W.C. Marshall	Year 5	K.S.C. Ng	Upper Sixth
A.J. Martin	Fifth	A.W. Nicholls	Shell
E.C. Martin	Upper Sixth	N.G. Oakley	Lower Sixth
L. Martin	Shell	P.C. Oakley	Remove
A. Martirossian	Year 5	A.J. O'Dell	Year 4
L. Martirossian	Year 7	T.P. O'Dell	Year 7
S.L. Masters	Shell	D.A.O. Odimayo	Upper Sixth
S.D. Masters	Year 7	U.C. Okolo	Upper Sixth
A.L. Maynard	Shell	E. Opare	Lower Sixth

C.E. Orfenov	Year 8	E.L. Rayner	Upper Sixth
O.E. Orfenov	Reception	T.E. Rayner	Lower Sixth
D.A. Osborn	Fifth	K.M. Reader	Fifth
E.J. O'Shea	Year 4	M.P. Reader	Year 8
L.G.M. O'Shea	Year 6	W. Reed	Upper Sixth
V.J. Ostwald	Upper Sixth	Y. Ren	Upper Sixth
E.C.L. Palmer	Year 1	A.W. Rhodes	Year 8
J.E. Palmer	Shell	K.H. Rick	Lower Sixth
Z.N.J. Palmer	Pre-Nursery	A.P.J.Rigden	Lower Sixth
A.S. Pang	Year 8	A.E. Riis	Shell
J.H.T. Pang	Year 6	L.M. Riis	Year 7
M. Pang	Lower Sixth	T.W. Riminton	Lower Sixth
E.P. Pangrazi	Year 3	P.E.H. Robathan	Lower Sixth
G.R. Pangrazi	Year 6	A.C.T. Roberts	Remove
B. Parker	Remove	J.H. Robertson	Shell
T.J. Parker	Remove	C.E. Rocks	Year 6
H.J.O. Parkinson	Remove	C.J. Roehrbein	Upper Sixth
C.J. Parsons	Fifth	E.S.E. Ross	Year 7
M.T.J. Payne	Year 8	J.A. Ross-Gower	Year 8
T.E. Perry	Reception	N.T. Rothblum	Lower Sixth
M. Pestalozza	Lower Sixth	W. Ruddle	Shell
C. Peter	Lower Sixth	J. Russ	Year 4
E.R. Phillips	Lower Sixth	Z. Russ	Year 3
I.R. Pierpoint	Year 4	E.L. Russell	Upper Sixth
F.J. Pilgrim	Year 7	O.S. Russell	Fifth
O.L.M. Pilgrim	Year 3	S.E. Russell	Fifth
J. Pin	Lower Sixth	M.E.J. Ruter	Lower Sixth
G.G.G. Pinkerton	Fifth	A.M. Rutherford	Fifth
C.D. Pinkney	Lower Sixth	A. Ruzicka	Upper Sixth
F.E. Pinks	Shell	H. Ryall	Shell
D.C. Pique	Upper Sixth	S. Safonov	Shell
V.K. Pitassi	Lower Sixth	A. Sakande	Year 8
A.D. Planterose	Year 2	N. Sakande	Fifth
H.L. Pockett	Shell	S. Samiullah	Upper Sixth
A.M.H. Pollard	Remove	E.W. Sanders	Remove
C.E.M. Pollard	Lower Sixth	L.E. Sanderson	Upper Sixth
S. Porthouse	Shell	M.G.B. Saxena	Year 7
S.C.D. Poynder	Year 8	M.M.A. Saxena	Year 5
T.J.M. Poynder	Year 8	A.W. Sayers	Year 2
A. Prasniewska	Remove	W. Sayers	Reception
M.R. Prest	Remove	I.V. Scharfenberg	Lower Sixth
C.J. Preston Bell	Lower Sixth	M. Schmid	Upper Sixth
H. Preston Bell	Remove	A.J.W. Schofield	Reception
G.R. Price	Remove	O.J. Schooling	Upper Sixth
F. Prinz	Upper Sixth	B.E. Scott	Remove
T.R. Prosser	Shell	E.R. Scutt	Fifth
B.J. Quelch	Year 1	M. Scutt	Year 8
H.D. Quelch	Year 3	S.J.R. Seager	Fifth
L.S. Quillien	Fifth	J.P. Searl	Year 7
M.H. Quinn	Year 6	S.C. Seeley	Lower Sixth
J. Rafferty	Year 8	E.V. Segal	Year 8
N.E. Rawbin	Year 7	I.L.Z. Segal	Year 6
R.J. Rawlinson	Upper Sixth	E. Seneviratne	Fifth

N. Serratosa Schulz	Remove	I.C.P. Tang	Fifth
O. Sharkey	Lower Sixth	X. Tang	Upper Sixth
A.G. Shaw	Nursery	C.W. Tapsell	Fifth
A.C. Shaw	Year 4	E.G. Taylor	Upper Sixth
N.A. Shaw	Year 5	J.G. Taylor	Year 8
L.J. Sheehan	Remove	A.T. Telford	Year 5
H. Shephard	Remove	L.K. Telford	Year 1
P. Shepilov	Lower Sixth	C. Terreni	Year 5
C. Silk	Lower Sixth	M. Terreni	Shell
M.E. Silk	Pre-Nursery	D.D.J. Thatcher	Shell
H.O. Sims	Remove	E.M.A. Thomas	Pre-Nursery
N.R. Slater	Fifth	O.W.J. Thomas	Year 1
D.W. Slattery	Fifth	M.M.K. Thompson	Pre-Nursery
A.A. Sleeper	Year 8	J.C. Thorne	Year 3
J.A.C. Sloane	Shell	R.L. Thorne	Year 6
R.J. Sloane	Fifth	C.M. Threadgold	Fifth
C.A. Smith	Lower Sixth	K.J. Threadgold	Lower Sixth
H.E. Smith	Upper Sixth	R. Tilford	Remove
P.A. Smith	Year 7	J.J. Tjong	Year 6
L.S. Smolinski	Upper Sixth	D.S.I. Tjong	Year 6
J.D. Smyth	Shell	L.J.I. Toleman	Nursery
M.V. Smyth	Upper Sixth	Z.O.R. Toleman	Year 1
K.H. Sorensen	Year 4	J. Tou	Lower Sixth
T.D.G. Sotiri	Remove	S. Trabucatti	Remove
O.R.A. Southgate	Year 8	V. Tsoi	Upper Sixth
C.A.J. Southwood	Year 7	D.W. Tuckwell	Upper Sixth
J.W.G. Southwood	Remove	R.C. Tuckwell	Fifth
L.C. Southwood	Lower Sixth	A.E. Turner	Fifth
S.A. Spector	Upper Sixth	J.J.M. Turner	Remove
T.H. Spector	Fifth	J. Turner	Year 8
E.C. Spiers	Year 4	H.W. Tye	Remove
J.J. Spuyman	Remove	G. Vans Agnew	Year 2
P.J. Spuyman	Year 6	H. Vans Agnew	Year 2
B.S. Stabler	Upper Sixth	T.M. Vans Agnew	Nursery
R. Stabler	Fifth	K. Vekaria	Remove
C.R. Stephenson	Shell	M.E. Venables	Lower Sixth
L.E. Stephenson	Year 8	H.D. Waddilove	Fifth
A.C. Stevens	Shell	H.G. Waddilove	Upper Sixth
H.M.D. Stevens	Fifth	E.P. Wade	Shell
J.I. Stevens	Upper Sixth	S.N. Wade	Fifth
E.A. Stoakes	Lower Sixth	T.M. Wade	Upper Sixth
S. Stollewerk	Lower Sixth	I.J.A. Walden	Year 5
T.S. Stone	Year 1	R.S.J. Walden	Shell
T. Storer	Year 7	J.A. Waller	Year 6
J.L. Strambi	Fifth	B.M. Wallis	Fifth
V. Swales	Remove	S.J. Walton	Reception
C. Swirski	Year 8	S. Walton	Year 3
E.R. Syed	Fifth	J.M. Wan	Lower Sixth
S.R. Syed	Shell	B.J. Ward	Year 1
E.A. Sykes	Year 5	C. Ward	Shell
S.W. Sykes	Year 3	C.C. Ward	Year 7
A.J. Taffinder	Remove	C.E.J. Ward	Lower Sixth
K. Tam	Lower Sixth	E.F. Ward	Remove

H.J. Ward	Year 4	J.R. Williams	Year 4
J.G. Ward	Year 8	J. Williams	Shell
K.P. Ward	Fifth	J. Williams	Shell
N.S.M. Ward	Upper Sixth	J. Williams	Shell
W.J. Ward	Year 5	L. Williams	Fifth
G.A. Waring	Year 8	R.C. Williams	Lower Sixth
O.A. Waring	Year 5	R.J. Williams	Fifth
E.G. Warwick	Year 5	S.R. Williams	Lower Sixth
W.E. Warwick	Shell	A.M. Willifer	Year 4
A. Waters	Year 6	A.E. Willifer	Year 6
I.C. Waters	Year 4	E.C. Wills	Upper Sixth
H.G. Wates	Remove	N.J. Wills	Remove
O.L.H. Watson	Remove	A.R.G. Wilson	Fifth
C.J. Watt	Upper Sixth	J.A.E. Wilson	Fifth
F.P. Watts	Fifth	O.T.S. Wilson	Year 7
T.R. Webb	Fifth	A. Wise	Fifth
K.A. Welch	Fifth	E.L. Wise	Lower Sixth
K.M. Welsh	Shell	T.L. Wise	Shell
I. Were	Year 7	G.C. Wolf	Upper Sixth
M. Were	Year 8	T.K. Wong	Year 8
J.C. Weston	Upper Sixth	T.J. Wood	Lower Sixth
T.H. Widdicombe	Year 8	T.R. Woodgate	Lower Sixth
C.T. Wilkins	Lower Sixth	E.E. Wright	Year 7
R. Wilkins	Shell	J.A. Wright	Remove
T.W. Wilkins	Upper Sixth	J.B. Wydra	Remove
A.E.K. Will	Remove	T.S. Yang	Remove
A.E. Willemse	Shell	K. Ye	Lower Sixth
E. Williams	Fifth	N. Zaitseva	Upper Sixth
H.C. Williams	Year 7		

Index

PICTURE ACKNOWLEDGEMENTS

Most of the pictures in the book come from the School Archives and from Old Ardinians. The Publisher would like to thank Emma Duggan for her photographs which appear at the start of each chapter and Andrea King for her help on the text and images. They would also like to thank Lancing College and Chapel for permission to reproduce a picture of Woodard's tomb on p19, the Mertens family on p24 and the carving of St Nicolas on p26 as well as Anne Drewery, the archivist at Lancing.

Finally, the Publisher would like to thank the following agencies for permission to use material: Corbis p18; Mary Evans Picture Library p24 (bottom), pp 92-93 *The Illustrated London News* and p35; Getty Images p44 (bottom), p134, pp139-40; Science and Society Picture Library p31 (top).